10575696

THE
International
Meat Book

ALSO BY CAROLE LALLI

Yesterday's Bread

Stuffings

Chicken Salads

THE
International
Meat Book

EDITED BY CAROLE LALLI

HarperCollins*Publishers*

THE INTERNATIONAL MEAT BOOK. Copyright © 2005 by HarperCollins Publishers Inc. All rights reserved. Printed in China. No part of this book may be used or reproduced in any manner whatsoever without written permission except in the case of brief quotations embodied in critical articles and reviews. For information, address HarperCollins Publishers Inc., 10 East 53rd Street, New York, NY 10022.

HarperCollins books may be purchased for educational, business, or sales promotional use. For information, please write: Special Markets Department, HarperCollins Publishers Inc., 10 East 53rd Street, New York, NY 10022.

FIRST EDITION

Designed by Jessica Shatan Heslin

Printed on acid-free paper

Library of Congress Cataloging-in-Publication Data

The international meat book / edited by Carole Lalli.
    p. cm.
ISBN 0-06-074283-6
1. Cookery (Meat) 2. Cookery, International   I. Lalli, Carole.

TX749.I58 2004
641.6'6—dc22

2004047386

05 06 07 08 09 ❖/TOP 10 9 8 7 6 5 4 3 2 1

Contents

Introduction   x

ONE   BEEF, VEAL, AND GAME

Grilled Porterhouse   2

Florentine Steak   4

Pepper Steak   5

Steak Marinated in Chianti   6

Rib Eye Steaks with Ha Cha Cha Sauce
and Frizzled Onions   8

Flank Steak with Oregon Blue Cheese
Sauce   10

Steak Verde with Crisp Pepper-Fried
Onion Shreds   12

Steaks with Tomato, Garlic, and Oregano
Sauce   15

Steak with Mushrooms and Marjoram   16

Beef Braised in Barolo   18

Beef and Potato Stew   20

Boiled Beef with Chili   22

Burgundy Beef   24

Sumatran Beef Curry   27

Stout-Braised Beef with Onions and Sour
Cream   30

Texas Short Ribs   32

Carne Guisada   34

New England Boiled Dinner   36

Provençal Pot-au-Feu   38

Fried Meatballs   41

Stuffed Beef Rolls   43

Stuffed Meat Loaf with *Salsa de Jitomate*   45

Ground Beef Salad   47

Waterfall Beef   49

Korean Barbecue   51

Best-of-the-Border Barbecue Brisket   53

Braised Veal Shanks with Lemon   56

Braised Veal Shank with Herbs   58

Veal Stew with Mushrooms and Peas   60

Calf's Liver and Bacon with Orange-Leek Sauce   62

Harvesters' Calf's Liver   64

Venison Stew with Prunes   66

Marinated Buffalo Steak   68

Buffalo Filet with Peppercorns and Mustard   70

TWO PORK

Pork with Rosemary   74

Roast Pork with Olives and Anchovies   76

Pork Tenderloin with Cranberry-Chipotle Sauce   78

Roast Leg of Pork in Adobo Sauce   80

Sweet and Savory Pork Leg with Rice   82

Catalonian Pork Brochettes   84

Skewered Pork Roasted with Malt Sugar   86

Meat Uruapan Style   88

Pork Curry   89

Pork Cutlets with Tapenade   90

Stuffed Pork Chops   92

Lemongrass Pork Chops   94

Cassoulet   95

Parsleyed Ham   98

Choucroute Garni   100

Pork with Sichuan Preserved Cabbage   102

Beef, Veal, and Game

Grilled Porterhouse

The name of this most popular steak comes from colonial America and its taverns, or "porter houses," where porters gathered to relax over dark ale. The cut comes from the thick end of the short loin and contains the T-bone and part of the tenderloin. Similar excellent cuts for grilling are the T-bone, club, tenderloin, and strip or shell steak. Names can change from region to region and can be confusing: in some places, a strip steak is called a New York steak or New York shell steak, but not in New York. For best taste, always look for prime beef, and, if possible, aged.

2½- to 3-pound porterhouse steak (or any of the other cuts mentioned above), about 2 inches thick
1 clove garlic, peeled and cut in half
2 teaspoons olive oil
Freshly ground pepper
Kosher or sea salt

Trim all but about ¼ inch of fat from the edges of the steak, then cut slashes about 1-inch apart in order to keep the steak from curling as it cooks. Pat the steak dry, rub both sides with the cut side of the garlic, brush it with the oil, and sprinkle it generously with the pepper. Let the steak stand at cool room temperature for 1 hour.

Prepare a charcoal grill or preheat a gas grill. Soak a few toothpicks in water.

When the fire is ready, secure the tail end of the steak with the toothpicks. Sprinkle the steak with salt and immediately place it on the grill. Sear for about 1 minute on both sides, then place it over medium-hot coals and grill for 6 to 7 minutes on each side for rare, 8 to 10 minutes for medium-rare. Depending on your grill, raise the rack and spread out the coals, or move the steak away from the hottest spot to control the temperature. If the fire flares, spray with water, or, if your grill has a cover, close it for just a moment, but do not cook the steak covered.

Remove the steak to a cutting board and let it rest for a few minutes before slicing. Cut the meat across the grain into slices about ¼ inch thick.

SERVES 4

Florentine Steak

Costata alla Fiorentina

I t is impossible to duplicate exactly the flavor of the beef used for the true version of this dish, which comes from the particular breed of cattle raised in the Val di Chiana, in Chianti, near Florence. But you will come close if you seek out the best prime, aged T-bone steaks and cook them over a wood-burning fire, though charcoal will do. If you use charcoal, choose a natural type rather than briquets.

2 T-bone steaks, about 2½ pounds each
2 tablespoons extra virgin olive oil
Salt
Freshly ground pepper

Brush the steaks with the olive oil and season to taste with the pepper. Let stand at room temperature for about 30 minutes.

Prepare a wood or charcoal fire.

When the fire is ready, sprinkle the steaks with salt and grill them for a total of about 15 minutes for medium-rare, or longer to taste. Remove the steaks to a cutting board and let them rest for 5 minutes. Slice the steaks and serve each person portions from each side of the bone.

SERVES 6

Pepper Steak

Steak au Poivre

The legend behind this dish is that around 1920, Emile Lerch, the chef at France's former royal Trianon Palace at Versailles, encrusted some tender but otherwise lackluster steaks in crushed black pepper to enliven their flavor. In short time, no respectable "Continental" menu was complete without *steak au poivre*. The dish became a bit of a cliché, but today *steak au poivre* has a kind of old-fashioned charm, especially for romantic dinners for two.

2 porterhouse steaks, 6 to 8 ounces each
Kosher or sea salt
1 to 2 tablespoons cracked—not
    ground—black peppercorns
4 tablespoons (½ stick) unsalted butter
2 tablespoons cognac or brandy
3 tablespoons *crème fraîche* or heavy
    cream

Pat the steaks dry and season them well with salt. Spread the peppercorns on a plate and press the steaks into them to coat each steak lightly on both sides.

Place a heavy skillet over high heat. Add half the butter and melt it. Add the steaks and cook for 2 to 3 minutes on each side. Pour in the cognac, and ignite. When the flames subside, remove the steaks from the pan and keep them warm on a plate.

Pour off the fat from the pan and add the cream. Bring to a simmer and whisk in the remaining 2 tablespoons butter until incorporated. Pour the sauce over the steaks and serve immediately.

SERVES 2

Steak Marinated in Chianti

Costata di Bue al Chianti

Chianti Classico, the underpinning of this dish, is aged for three years or longer, which gives it a full-bodied, fruity flavor. Unlike the traditional grilled Florentine steak (see page 4), the steaks for this dish are considerably thinner.

3 T-bone steaks, about 1¼ pounds each

1 carrot, coarsely chopped

1 yellow onion, coarsely chopped

1 celery stalk, coarsely chopped

2 bay leaves

1 tablespoon juniper berries

1 (24-ounce) bottle good-quality
    Chianti Classico

2 tablespoons extra virgin olive oil

Salt

Freshly ground pepper

Place the steaks in a single layer in a large glass or porcelain (nonmetal) dish. Add the carrot, onion, celery, bay leaves, and juniper berries. Pour in the Chianti, cover, and place the dish in the refrigerator for about 12 hours.

Remove the steaks from the marinade and pat them dry. Pour the marinade into a saucepan set over medium heat. Bring the marinade to a simmer and cook until it is reduced by one-fourth, about 1 hour. Discard the bay leaves and pass the marinade through a food mill set over a saucepan. Or puree the marinade in a food processor or blender. Transfer the marinade to a saucepan.

Meanwhile, prepare a charcoal fire or preheat the broiler. Warm the sauce over medium heat. When the fire is ready, brush the steaks with the olive oil and season with salt and pepper. Grill the steaks for about 1½ minutes on each side for medium-rare, or longer according to taste. Transfer the steaks to a warm platter and pour the warm sauce over or pass it separately at the table.

SERVES 6

Rib Eye Steaks with Ha Cha Cha Sauce and Frizzled Onions

This recipe comes from the Driftwood Ranch on Orcas Island off the Pacific Northwest, home to a prize herd of Charolais cattle. The steaks also can be grilled over charcoal and the sauce served separately.

FOR THE SAUCE

1 tablespoon peanut oil

1 onion, peeled and chopped

8 cloves garlic, peeled and crushed

2 cups good-quality crushed or chopped
   canned tomatoes

⅓ cup dark molasses

½ cup packed brown sugar

½ cup red wine vinegar

1 dried ancho or poblano chili, ground

½ teaspoon ground cinnamon

¼ teaspoon ground cloves

1 teaspoon ground cumin

1 teaspoon freshly ground black pepper

1 teaspoon paprika

½ teaspoon cayenne pepper

1 teaspoon salt

FOR THE STEAKS

Peanut oil for frying

6 medium rib eye steaks

Salt

Freshly ground pepper

FOR THE ONIONS

1 cup flour

1 teaspoon salt

1 teaspoon cornstarch

2 large red onions, peeled and sliced into
   ⅛-inch rings

Make the barbecue sauce: Place a small saucepan over medium heat. Add the oil and when hot, add the onion and garlic; sauté until the onion is translucent, about 5 minutes. Add all the remaining sauce ingredients and simmer over low heat for 30 minutes. Remove from the heat and keep warm.

To prepare the steaks, heat 1 tablespoon of peanut oil in a large skillet over high heat. Season the steaks on both sides with salt and pepper. Put them in the skillet and cook for 3 minutes on each side for medium-rare, or until the meat springs back when touched. Baste the steaks while they cook with a bit of the barbecue sauce. If your skillet is not large enough to accommodate the steaks, cook them in two batches or in two skillets. Remove from the heat and keep warm.

Pour peanut oil to a depth of 3 to 4 inches into a wide, deep, heavy pan and heat to 350°F on a deep-fat thermometer. Mix the flour, salt, and cornstarch together in a medium bowl. Dredge the onion rings in the flour mixture, shaking off the excess. Carefully drop the rings into the hot oil. Fry the rings until golden, about 5 minutes.

Serve the steaks on a platter surrounded by the onions, and pass the remaining barbecue sauce at the table.

SERVES 6

Flank Steak with Oregon Blue Cheese Sauce

A London broil with a Northwest twist, this flank steak departs from the usual barbecue fare. To maintain the theme, serve it with crusty sourdough bread, a salad, and a lush Pinot Noir from the region.

3 pounds flank steak, trimmed
¼ cup cracked black pepper
¼ cup chopped garlic
6 bay leaves, fresh if possible
1 tablespoon fresh chopped rosemary
¾ cup Oregon or other good Pinot Noir
2 tablespoons olive oil
1 tablespoon red wine vinegar
1 cup homemade or good-quality commercial beef broth
3 tablespoons unsalted butter, softened
3 tablespoons flour
Salt
Freshly ground pepper
8 ounces Oregon blue cheese or other mild blue cheese, crumbled (about 2 cups loosely packed)
Fresh watercress for garnish

Rub the steak with the cracked pepper and garlic and place it in a shallow glass or stainless steel dish. Add the bay leaves, rosemary, wine, olive oil, and vinegar. Cover and refrigerate for 24 hours, turning the meat 2 or 3 times.

Prepare a charcoal fire. Remove the meat from the refrigerator 30 minutes before cooking.

Remove the meat from the marinade and pat it dry with a towel. Strain the marinade into a medium nonreactive saucepan and discard the herbs and spices. Bring the liquid to a low boil and continue boiling until it is reduced by half. Add the beef broth to the wine reduction and bring to a simmer.

Make a *beurre manié* by combining the butter with the flour, incorporating it completely. In small bits, whisk the butter-flour mixture into the wine mixture, whisking well after each addition until a

smooth sauce of the desired thickness has been achieved. Season to taste with salt and pepper and keep warm over very low heat.

Season the steak generously with salt and pepper and grill it over medium-hot coals for 3 minutes per side. Then turn and cook again on each side for 3 minutes for a total cooking time of 12 minutes for medium-rare. For medium, cook 1 minute longer on each side, for a total of 14 minutes.

Transfer the meat to a warm serving platter and let it rest in a warm spot.

Remove the sauce from the heat and whisk in 1½ cups of the blue cheese, stirring until smooth. Check the seasoning and adjust with salt and pepper as necessary. Cut the steak on the diagonal across the grain into ¼-inch slices and arrange on a platter. Top with the sauce and garnish with the watercress and the remaining cheese.

SERVES 6 TO 8

Steak Verde with Crisp Pepper-Fried Onion Shreds

Here is one more showcase for the food that made Texas famous. The slow heat and richness of the meat are sharpened by the spicy onions. Tiny potatoes roasted with rosemary are all you need to complete the menu. The roasted poblano chilies called for can be found in the Mexican food section of a well-stocked supermarket, or see below to roast fresh ones.

2 large sweet onions, such as Texas 1015
    Supersweet or Vidalia
2 cups buttermilk
1 cup flour
3 tablespoons yellow cornmeal
1 teaspoon paprika
¼ teaspoon ground cumin
¼ teaspoon cayenne pepper
Big pinch freshly ground black pepper
1 tablespoon chili powder
Salt to taste
1 whole beef filet, 4 to 5 pounds,
    trimmed of all fat and sinew

Coarsely cracked peppercorns
¼ cup olive oil or 4 tablespoons (½ stick)
    unsalted butter
¼ to ½ cup roasted garlic, mashed
    (about 2 heads, see Notes)
1 red onion, thinly sliced
3 cups shredded Monterey Jack cheese
    with jalapeño pepper
2 cups chopped roasted green poblano
    chilies (see Notes)
2 tablespoons fresh rosemary leaves
2 tablespoons fresh oregano leaves
Vegetable oil for deep-frying

Using a mandoline or a food processor fitted with the fine slicing blade, finely slice the sweet onions. Separate them into rings and place them in a medium bowl. Pour in the buttermilk and set aside for 1 hour. Combine all the following ingredients, up to the beef, in a plastic bag and shake to combine well. Set the bag aside until needed.

Preheat the oven to 500°F. Season the beef with the peppercorns to taste, rubbing them over the surface. Place a large, heavy frying pan or sauté pan over medium-high heat and add the oil to warm. Place the filet in the pan and brown it evenly, turning. Remove to a platter to cool slightly.

Using a small sharp knife, make 6 cuts crosswise about 1½ inches deep every 2 inches along the length of the filet. Line each cut with equal amounts of the mashed roasted garlic. Push half the red onion, cheese, chilies, rosemary, and oregano into each cut.

Place the filet on a rack in a roasting pan and place it in the oven. Immediately reduce the heat to 350°F. Roast the meat until it is done to your taste—about 30 minutes for rare, or to 125°F on an instant-read thermometer.

Preheat the broiler.

Remove the meat from the oven and top it with the remaining red onion slices, cheese, chilies, rosemary, and oregano. Place the meat under the broiler until the cheese melts, just a few minutes. Remove the meat from the broiler, cover it loosely with aluminum foil, and let it rest in a warm spot for 10 minutes.

Drain the onion rings in a colander. Place a deep-fryer or saucepan over medium-high heat and pour in oil to a depth of 2 inches. Heat to 365°F on a deep-fat thermometer, or until a tiny bit of bread begins to brown within moments of being dropped in the oil.

Working in batches, drop the onion shreds into the flour mixture in the plastic bag, coating them and then shaking off the excess. Drop the floured onions into the hot oil, stirring until golden brown, 2 to 3 minutes. Remove the onions with a slotted spoon and transfer them to paper towels to drain briefly. Sprinkle the onions to taste with salt.

Place the filet on a platter, surround it with the crisp-fried onion shreds, and serve immediately.

SERVES 10

NOTE To roast garlic, place cloves on a Mexican *comal* (see page 81), griddle, or cast-iron skillet over medium-high heat until the skin is charred. Alternatively, preheat the oven to 450°F, wrap whole heads of garlic in heavy-duty foil and place them in the oven. Roast until a clove is tender when pierced with a cake tester or toothpick.

NOTE To roast peppers, place them over the flame or gas plate on a stovetop. Turn the peppers as the skin chars, then, once they are charred all over, place them in a plastic or paper bag and close tightly. Remove the skins once the peppers are cool enough to handle.

Steaks with Tomato, Garlic, and Oregano Sauce

Braciole alla Pizzaiola

Steak *pizzaiola*—in other words, in the style of the pizza maker—refers to the familiar and enduringly appealing combination of tomato, garlic, oregano, and for some, Neapolitans in particular, anchovies. For this dish, use thin, wide boneless slices of steak, such as sirloin or rib. Some butchers or Italian markets sell "beef for braciole."

¼ cup extra virgin olive oil

6 thin slices beef, about ½ inch thick and 6 ounces each (see Headnote)

2 cloves garlic, peeled and roughly chopped

4 anchovy fillets, chopped, optional

1 pound fresh ripe tomatoes, peeled, seeded, and coarsely chopped, or 2 cups best-quality Italian whole canned tomatoes, well drained and chopped

Salt

Freshly ground pepper

¼ cup loosely packed fresh oregano leaves, or 2 teaspoons dried, or 2 tablespoons fresh Italian parsley leaves

Heat the oil in a cast-iron skillet over high heat large enough to hold all the meat in one layer, or, if necessary, work in batches. Add the meat and cook quickly until just lightly browned on both sides. Remove the meat to a platter.

Reduce the heat to medium. Add the garlic and anchovies, if using, and cook, stirring, for a minute or so, until the garlic is golden brown. Do not let the garlic burn or the sauce will be bitter. Add the tomatoes and season to taste with salt and a generous grinding of pepper. Reduce the heat and cook the sauce, stirring, for about 3 minutes. Stir in the oregano, return the meat and any accumulated juices to the sauce, and cook for 1 to 2 minutes longer, while spooning the sauce over the meat. Adjust the seasonings and serve at once.

SERVES 6

Steak with Mushrooms and Marjoram

Bistecca alla Cacciatora

Cacciatora in Italian means a hunter or woodsman. When the word is applied to a dish, it generally indicates one that includes mushrooms. This particular preparation boasts marjoram, too, which grows wild along the coast of Grosseto, the southernmost province of Tuscany.

1 ounce dried porcini mushrooms

2 tablespoons extra virgin olive oil

2 cloves garlic, peeled and chopped

6 thin flank (rump) steaks, about 6
    ounces each

1 cup dry red wine

1 tablespoon tomato paste

1 tablespoon fresh marjoram leaves, or
    1 teaspoon dried

1 tablespoon juniper berries

Salt

Freshly ground pepper

Place the mushrooms in a small bowl, cover with tepid water, and let soak for 30 minutes. Drain the mushrooms over a cup and reserve the liquid. If the liquid seems gritty, strain it again through a small strainer lined with cheesecloth or a coffee filter. Squeeze the mushrooms of excess liquid and chop them coarsely.

Place a skillet large enough to hold the steaks in one layer over medium heat. Add the olive oil and heat until warm. Add the garlic and stir for about 30 seconds. Add the steaks and cook to brown, about 2 minutes on each side. Remove the steaks to a platter and let them rest in a warm spot.

Lower the heat and add the wine, tomato paste, marjoram, juniper berries, and mushrooms. Season to taste with salt and pepper and cook, stirring, for about 5 minutes. Return the steaks and any accumulated juices to the pan and cook for about 5 minutes. Add the reserved mushroom soaking liquid as needed if the pan becomes too dry—the sauce should not be too thick.

Serve the steaks at once, topped with the mushroom sauce on a platter.

Beef Braised in Barolo

Stracotto al Barolo

Barolo—one of the glorious wines from Piedmont—is the underpinning of this dish, and it will be best made if you select a bottle that is at least five years old. That is not so old for Barolo, and the result will be a tastier, more viscous sauce.

2 pounds boneless beef for braising, such as chuck or bottom round

2 medium carrots, trimmed, scrubbed, and roughly chopped

1 medium onion, peeled and roughly chopped

2 celery stalks, trimmed and roughly chopped

1 cup Italian parsley sprigs

2 bay leaves, fresh if possible

1 tablespoon juniper berries

1 teaspoon peppercorns

1½ cups aged Barolo wine

½ cup diced fresh pork fat or lard

1 tablespoon extra virgin olive oil

1 tablespoon butter

Salt

Freshly ground pepper

Place the meat in a deep nonreactive bowl that will accommodate it comfortably and add all the following ingredients up to the lard. Cover the bowl and refrigerate to marinate for at least 24 hours.

When ready to cook, remove the bowl from the refrigerator, remove the beef from the marinade, and pat it dry with paper towels. Strain the vegetables from the wine, and reserve the wine. Using a small sharp knife, make cuts along the surface of the meat, then insert bits of lard or pork fat into the cuts.

Preheat the oven to 350°F. Place a heavy pot or Dutch oven over medium-high heat and add the olive oil and butter. When the butter stops foaming, sprinkle the meat generously with salt and add it to the pot. Brown the meat thoroughly on all sides, adjusting the heat to keep the fat hot but preventing it from burning.

Add the vegetables to the pot and stir briefly to coat with the fat. Add 1 cup of the reserved wine, cover the pot, and place it in the oven. Cook the meat for about 3 hours, or until it is tender when tested with a thin sharp knife or cake tester. Turn the meat several times while cooking; add wine if necessary as the liquid is absorbed, and adjust the oven heat to maintain a low simmer.

With a slotted spoon, remove the meat to a warm platter and cover it loosely with foil. Put the wine and vegetables from the pot through a food mill or process to a rough puree in a food processor. Transfer to a saucepan and warm the sauce over medium heat. Meanwhile, cut the meat into slices about ¼ inch thick and arrange on a serving platter. Pour the sauce over the meat and serve at once.

SERVES 6

Beef and Potato Stew

Boeuf à la Gardiane

In the Camargue, in Provence, this is known as *boeuf à la gardiane* after the *gardians,* the horsemen who look after the bulls and horses. Apparently, cowboys gravitate to the same sort of hearty, no-nonsense fare on whatever range they roam.

2 pounds stewing beef
Salt
2 tablespoons olive oil
¼ pound lean salt pork, cut into
    lardoons about 1 inch by ¼ inch
1 large onion, peeled and chopped
3 cloves garlic, peeled and crushed
Boiling water
Bouquet garni of a few sprigs Italian
    parsley, fresh thyme, bay leaf, and a
    3-inch strip dried orange peel, tied
    with kitchen twine or in cheesecloth
1 pound baking potatoes, peeled and
    sliced ¼ inch thick
⅔ cup black olives, such as niçoises,
    pitted and coarsely chopped
Freshly ground pepper

Pat the beef with paper towels to remove excess moisture and sprinkle it all over with salt. Warm the olive oil in a large, heavy sauté pan over medium-high heat. Add the beef and brown it well all over, turning with a wooden spoon. Do not crowd the pan; if the meat does not fit all at once, brown it in batches, adjusting the heat to keep the pan from burning. It will take about 15 minutes to brown all the meat.

Add the salt pork and cook, stirring, until lightly colored, about 6 minutes. Return all the beef to the pan. Add the onion, lower the heat, and cook, stirring, until lightly browned, about 5 minutes. Add the garlic and 1 cup boiling water and deglaze the pan, scraping the bottom with the spoon until the browned bits dissolve. Tuck the bouquet garni into the center of the pan, cover the meat with the sliced potatoes, and pour additional boiling water over until the potatoes are nearly covered.

Cover the pan and cook over the lowest possible heat until the meat and

the potatoes are quite tender—the potatoes should be nearly falling apart, 2½ to 3 hours. Stir in the olives about 5 minutes before the dish is done and grind a generous amount of pepper over the top.

SERVES 4 TO 6

Boiled Beef with Chili

This Sichuan specialty displays the typical and often seemingly contradictory characteristics of the region's cooking. It is at once hot and spicy as well as tender and rich almost to the point of being heavy. The dish is delicious, and, clearly, complex. In Sichuan Province, cooks often prepared beef in a broth seasoned with chili peppers, bean paste, and pepper.

2 tablespoons lard or vegetable oil

6 dried red chilies

1½ teaspoons Sichuan peppercorns, ground, optional

1 tablespoon fermented black beans, finely chopped

3 cloves garlic, peeled and finely chopped, plus 1 teaspoon for finishing, optional

3 to 4 slices fresh ginger, finely chopped

6 to 8 scallions, trimmed and chopped, white parts only

1 tablespoon hot bean paste

10 ounces beef steak, such as sirloin, cut into paper-thin slices

6 to 8 lettuce leaves, washed and torn into small pieces

1 tablespoon hot chili oil

Heat the lard in a wok or skillet and fry the dried chilies and 1 teaspoon ground Sichuan peppercorns (if using) for about 30 seconds; remove and chop the chilies finely. Add the black beans to the wok and fry them for about 30 seconds. Add the garlic, ginger, scallions, and the bean paste and stir-fry together until aromatic, 1 to 2 minutes. Return the chilies and pepper to the wok, add ½ cup water, and bring just to a boil. Set the sauce aside.

Bring a large saucepan of water to a boil. Add the beef and cook very briefly, stirring with a wooden spoon, until it just loses its color. Immediately drain the meat well.

Add the meat to the the sauce in the wok, reheat, and stir-fry until all the sauce has coated the slices. Stir in the lettuce.

Transfer the mixture to a serving platter, and splash on the hot oil. Sprinkle on the remaining ground Sichuan pepper and the additional chopped garlic, if using, and serve at once.

SERVES 2 TO 4

Burgundy Beef

Boeuf à la Bourguignonne

This is unarguably one of the greatest of all beef stews and a hallmark of French provincial cooking. Serve it with plain boiled potatoes or buttered noodles.

½ pound salt pork, skin removed

3 tablespoons or more vegetable oil

3½ to 4 pounds stewing beef, in 2-inch cubes

Salt

Freshly ground pepper

3 tablespoons unsalted butter

2 medium carrots, peeled and sliced

1 medium onion, peeled and chopped

2 cloves garlic, peeled and crushed

2 tablespoons flour

3 tablespoons marc de Bourgogne or brandy

3 cups (24-ounce bottle) red Burgundy wine

1 to 2 bay leaves, depending on size, fresh if possible

3 sprigs fresh thyme

36 pearl onions, peeled (see Note)

36 small white cultivated mushrooms or larger mushrooms

1 tablespoon lemon juice

About 2 tablespoons chopped Italian parsley leaves for garnish

Bring a medium pot of water to the boil. Cut the salt pork into lardoons about 1½ inches long and about ½ inch thick. Drop the pork into the boiling water and boil for about 10 minutes; drain, refresh well under cold water, and set aside.

Heat 1 tablespoon of the oil in a heavy 6-quart pot or Dutch oven. Pat the lardoons dry with paper towels and place them in the pot; cook over low heat, stirring, until the pork is golden brown, about 5 minutes. Remove the pork from the pot and set it aside.

Dry the beef cubes well with paper towels and season with salt and pepper. Raise the heat to medium-high and add 1 tablespoon

of the butter to the pot. Add the beef. Without crowding, brown the meat well on all sides; do this in batches, if necessary, and adjust the heat to keep the bottom of the pot from burning. Add vegetable oil, if necessary. Remove the beef as it browns, adding it to the pork. Remove all but about 2 tablespoons of fat from the pot.

Add the carrots, onion, and garlic to the pot and cook over medium heat, stirring, for about 5 minutes, until the vegetables are softened and lightly browned; do not let them burn. Return the meat to the pot. Sprinkle in the flour and stir to cover

the ingredients evenly. Cook over medium heat, stirring constantly, for about 2 minutes. Pour the marc, then the wine into the pot and continue stirring and scraping up any browned bits from the bottom. Add the bay leaves and 2 sprigs of thyme. Raise the heat, and when the liquid just begins to bubble, cover the pot, reduce the heat to very low, and cook for 2 hours or longer, until the meat is tender. Stir from time to time and adjust the heat as needed to maintain a low simmer. (You also can do this in a preheated oven, 325°F or 350°F, again taking care to maintain a low simmer.)

Meanwhile, prepare the onions and mushrooms. Place a medium sauté pan over medium heat, and add a tablespoon of butter and a teaspoon of oil. When the butter stops foaming, add the peeled onions, a pinch of salt, pepper and the remaining sprig thyme. Cook the onions over low heat, turning from time to time, until they are golden brown, about 10 minutes (they will not be evenly colored). Set the onions aside, discard the thyme, and wipe the pan clean.

Trim the mushroom stems, brush or wipe the caps clean if necessary, and cut medium or large ones in half or in quarters. Add the remaining butter and a teaspoon of oil to the sauté pan set over medium-high heat. Add the mushrooms, season with salt, pepper, and the lemon juice. Cook rapidly, stirring, until the mushrooms are browned and no longer exuding juice. Add the mushrooms to the onions.

About 20 minutes before you think the meat is fork-tender but not falling apart, add the onions and mushrooms to the pot. Continue cooking, stirring once or twice, until the ingredients are cooked through. Or set aside to reheat just before serving. At this point, you may also want to adjust the sauce. If you prefer a thicker sauce, remove the meat and vegetables with a slotted spoon or drain them over a bowl through a colander, return the sauce to the pan, and reduce over medium-high heat to the desired consistency. Return the meat and vegetables to the pot and heat through. Sprinkle with the parsley and serve.

SERVES 8

NOTE An efficient way to peel the onions is to drop them into a pot of rapidly boiling water and let them boil for about 1 minute. Drain the onions and then plunge them immediately into a bowl of ice water. The skins should slip off easily or with just a bit of assistance from a sharp paring knife.

Sumatran Beef Curry

Kelia Sumatera

Sumatran dishes are heavy with spices, fragrant with fresh herbs, and burning hot with chili and pepper, for this is food from the original Spice Islands. Beef or young buffalo, poultry, organ meats, and seafood are the ingredients typically used in curries like this one.

4 large onions, peeled and coarsely chopped
8 cloves garlic, peeled and coarsely chopped
1½-inch piece fresh ginger, peeled and chopped
1 stalk lemongrass, lower pale root section only, peeled and minced
2 to 3 tablespoons vegetable oil
2 pounds beef for braising, such as shank, flank, or chuck steak, cubed
1 tablespoon ground coriander
2 tablespoons ground cumin

¾ teaspoon turmeric
¾ teaspoon Asian shrimp paste
2 cups thin unsweetened coconut milk
2 Kaffir lime leaves or bay leaves, fresh if possible
2 to 3 fresh red chili peppers
8 candlenuts or macadamia nuts, or 24 raw cashews
Salt
10 small new potatoes
2 tablespoons chopped scallions, optional
Hot cooked white rice

Place the onions, garlic, ginger and lemongrass in the work bowl of a food processor or in a blender and process to a puree.

Heat the oil in a heavy saucepan over medium-high heat. Pat the meat to dry it well, then brown it evenly in the oil. Remove the meat as it browns to a bowl and set it aside. Add the onion puree to the pot and cook, stirring frequently, for 5 minutes. Add the spices and shrimp paste and cook briefly. Add the coconut milk and lime leaves, bring the mixture just to the boil, lower the heat, and simmer for 5 minutes.

Trim the chilies, halve them lengthwise, and scrape out the seeds. Add the flesh to the curry mixture in the pot. Grind the nuts to a powder and stir the powder into the sauce. Add salt to taste. Return the meat to the pot and cook at a gentle simmer for 1½ hours, until the meat is very tender. If the sauce becomes very thick, add additional coconut milk or water during cooking.

Peel the potatoes and, after the curry has cooked for about 1 hour, add them, cooking until they are tender and the sauce is thick. Garnish with the scallions, if desired, and serve with the rice.

SERVES 6 TO 8

Stout-Braised Beef with Onions and Sour Cream

Braising, the process of long slow cooking that results in tender meat and complex flavor, is particularly successful here. The hearty stout, sweet onions, and spicy accents of mustard and allspice meld into a unique sauce that will be even better if you can manage to prepare this stew a day or two in advance. Serve it with egg noodles or steamed new potatoes.

4 strips bacon, cut into 1-inch pieces

1 cup flour

2 tablespoons salt

1 tablespoon freshly ground white
   pepper

1 tablespoon ground allspice

3 pounds beef sirloin tips or sirloin
   roast, cut into 2½ by ½ by ½-inch
   pieces

2 large yellow onions, cut into thin
   wedges

1 teaspoon sugar

1½ cups stout

4 cups homemade or best-quality store-
   bought beef broth

¼ cup Dijon mustard

1 cup sour cream

1 cup finely sliced scallions, white parts
   only

Place a large, heavy saucepan or Dutch oven over medium heat, add the bacon and cook until lightly browned, 7 to 10 minutes. Remove and discard the bacon.

Meanwhile, combine the flour, salt, white pepper, and allspice. Dry the pieces of meat with paper towels, then dredge them well in the flour mixture, shaking off the excess. Add the pieces of meat, in batches if necessary to avoid crowding, to the pan and brown well. Remove the meat to a bowl as it browns.

Add the onions and sugar to the pan and cook until the onions are translucent, about 5 minutes. Return the browned meat and any accumulated juices to the pan. Stir in the stout, broth, and mustard and bring the liquid to a simmer. Reduce the heat to medium-low and skim the surface of any fat. Season with salt and pepper.

Cover the pan and cook for 2 to 3 hours, until the meat is fork-tender, stirring from time to time and adjusting the heat to maintain just a low simmer. If prepared in advance, let the stew cool to room temperature, then cover and refrigerate. When ready to serve, remove any fat from the surface; let the stew return to room temperature before reheating slowly.

Just before serving, top the stew with the sour cream and sprinkle over the scallions.

SERVES 6 TO 8

Texas Short Ribs

Short ribs and flanken are cut ends of the rib roast, the flanken coming from the underside. These cuts are tender when braised or stewed as in this preparation, but also contain quite a bit of fat. Cooking this and similar dishes a day in advance not only develops the flavors nicely, but with overnight refrigeration also allows the fat to rise to the top and solidify, which makes removing it easy.

½ cup flour
Salt
Freshly ground pepper
¼ teaspoon ground allspice
3 to 3½ pounds beef short ribs (or flanken or brisket or top skirt steak)
4 tablespoons (½ stick) unsalted butter
1 tablespoon vegetable oil
2 large onions, peeled and chopped
2 cloves garlic, peeled and chopped
1 small jalapeño pepper, seeded, deveined, and minced

1 small green bell pepper, seeded and chopped
1 celery stalk, chopped
2 tablespoons brown sugar
½ teaspoon sweet paprika
2 tablespoons chili powder
½ teaspoon dry mustard
¼ cup lemon juice
½ cup prepared (store-bought) chili sauce
½ cup dark beer or ale
1 (17-ounce) can chopped tomatoes
Chopped fresh parsley

Preheat the oven to 350F. Combine the flour with ½ teaspoon salt, ½ teaspoon pepper, and the allspice on a large plate or sheet of waxed paper. Set 1 tablespoon of the mixture aside. Wipe the short ribs dry and roll them in the flour mixture, patting it onto the meat and shaking off the excess.

Place a large, heavy pot or Dutch oven over medium-high heat. Add 3 tablespoons of the butter and the oil and heat.

Add the ribs, a few at a time, and brown them well on all sides. As they brown, transfer them to a plate.

Reduce the heat to medium and add the remaining 1 tablespoon butter to the pot. Stir in the onions, garlic, and peppers, scraping the bottom and sides of the pot. Cook, stirring occasionally, for 5 minutes. Sprinkle in the reserved tablespoon of seasoned flour mixture and cook 2 minutes, stirring.

Add the celery, brown sugar, paprika, chili powder, mustard, lemon juice, chili sauce, and beer, stir well, and add the tomatoes. Return the ribs to the pot and heat to boil-ing. Cover and transfer to the oven. Bake for 1½ hours, turning the meat once and taking care to maintain the liquid just at a simmer; lower the heat if necessary. Uncover and bake for 15 minutes longer.

Skim the fat and serve, sprinkled with the parsley. Or, let the dish come to room temperature and refrigerate for up to 2 days. When ready to serve, remove the fat, which will have risen to the surface and become firm, then allow the contents to reach room temperature before slowly reheating.

SERVES 6

Carne Guisada

This popular dish made its way from Mexico into Texas, where it is often served with refried beans and sliced tomatoes topped with creamy guacamole alongside hot flour tortillas. Jalapeños are always an option for added heat. In south Texas, this stew often shows up wrapped in flour tortillas, as a hearty, portable breakfast.

3 tablespoons vegetable oil

2 pounds beef round steak, cut into 1-inch cubes

2 tablespoons flour

½ green bell pepper, seeded and finely chopped

½ yellow onion, peeled and finely chopped

1 large tomato, finely chopped

1 fresh jalapeño pepper, thinly sliced crosswise

3 cloves garlic, peeled and finely chopped

½ teaspoon ground cumin

1 teaspoon chili powder

½ teaspoon salt

¼ teaspoon freshly ground pepper

½ cup beef broth or water, or more as needed

Place a large saucepan or heavy pot or Dutch oven over medium-high heat and add the oil. Pat the beef cubes dry with paper towels and add them to the hot oil, in batches if necessary, to avoid crowding. Remove the meat to a bowl when lightly brown. Return all the meat to the pan, sprinkle it with the flour, and add the bell pepper, onion, and tomato. Stir well, and add the jalapeño, garlic, cumin, chili powder, salt, pepper, and broth.

Reduce the heat to low, cover, and simmer gently until the meat is very tender, 2 to 2½ hours. Stir from time to time, and adjust the heat as needed to maintain a very low simmer. Add additional broth or water if the stew begins to stick to the bottom of the pan.

SERVES 4 TO 6

New England Boiled Dinner

Known throughout the colonies, boiled dinner, like this New Hampshire version, could be put on the stove in the morning and be ready for dinner, which was the midday meal. Salt, pickled, or "corned" beef was the centerpiece, and the leftovers, tinted by the beets, became red flannel hash for the following day's breakfast.

1 corned beef brisket (salt beef), about
   3 pounds
12 small or slender carrots, peeled
6 small turnips, peeled
6 medium all-purpose potatoes, peeled
8 small beets, trimmed but not peeled
1 small head cabbage, roughly chopped
1½ tablespoons unsalted butter
1½ tablespoons flour
1½ tablespoons dry mustard
1 teaspoon Dijon mustard
1 tablespoon red wine vinegar
½ cup sour cream, at room temperature
Salt
Freshly ground pepper

Rinse the meat with cold water and place it in a large, heavy pot or Dutch oven. Cover the meat with cold water, place the pot over medium-high heat, and bring to a boil, skimming the surface as necessary. Reduce the heat, cover, and simmer for 2½ hours.

Add the carrots, turnips, and potatoes to the pot and continue to simmer, covered, until the vegetables and meat are tender, about 40 minutes longer.

Meanwhile, place the beets in a saucepan and cover with cold water. Heat to boiling; reduce the heat and simmer, uncovered, until tender, about 30 minutes. Immediately refresh under cold running water. Peel the beets and place them in a bowl; keep them in a warm spot or in a warming oven.

When the beets have cooked for about 15 minutes, place the cabbage in a saucepan. Remove ½ cup of the liquid from the pot containing the corned beef and pour it over the cabbage. Heat to boiling, reduce the heat, and cook, partially covered, until the cabbage is just tender and all the liquid has evaporated, about 15 minutes. Remove the cover if the cabbage is cooking too quickly to absorb the liquid. Reduce the heat to low and keep warm.

When the corned beef is tender, transfer it to a heatproof platter and place the vegetables in a heatproof bowl. Cover the platter and bowl loosely with foil and place them in a warming oven. Reserve the cooking liquid.

Melt the butter in a saucepan over low heat. Stir in the flour and both mustards. Cook, stirring constantly, for 3 minutes. Whisk in 1½ cups of the reserved corned beef cooking liquid and the vinegar. Heat to boiling and boil until slightly thickened, about 4 minutes. Remove from the heat, whisk in the sour cream, and warm slightly. Add salt and pepper to taste and spoon into a sauce dish.

To serve, slice the meat and arrange it on the platter. Surround the meat with the carrots, potatoes, and turnips. Serve the cabbage and beets in separate bowls. Pass the sauce at the table.

SERVES 6

Provençal Pot-au-Feu

Pot-au-Feu à la Provençale

A Provençal pot-au-feu is distinguished by the presence, in addition to the usual beef cuts, of a lamb shank, which lends complexity to the flavor and softness to the texture of the broth. The famous gastronome Austin de Croze, writing in 1928, claims that it is obligatory to accompany a Provençal pot-au-feu with a warm chickpea salad. He is often quoted but rarely respected.

1 pig's foot (trotter)

3 pounds boned beef shank, in a single piece

1½ pounds beef short ribs

1 lamb shank, about 1½ pounds

1 large beef marrowbone, 1½ to 2 pounds, tied in cheesecloth

½ cup dry white wine

Handful of kosher or sea salt

1 large onion, peeled and stuck with 2 whole cloves

1 whole head garlic

Large bouquet garni of 2 bay leaves, 6 sprigs thyme, and 10 sprigs parsley

1 pound young, tender carrots, peeled

1 pound small crisp turnips, peeled

2 pounds leeks

6 slices semi-stale bread

Coarse sea salt, capers, and picholine or niçoise olives for serving

Place the pig's foot in a medium saucepan, add cold water to cover, and bring to a full boil. Drain, rinse under cold water, drain again, and set aside.

Using kitchen twine, tie the beef shank and short ribs together in a compact package. In a traditional earthenware pot-au-feu or deep, heavy flameproof casserole or Dutch oven, arrange all the meats, including the pig's foot. The meats should not be tightly packed, but there also should not be an excess of space among the pieces.

Pour in cold water to cover the meat by about 2 inches and place the pot over low-to-medium heat, protected from direct heat by a heat diffuser if one is available. Bring the water very slowly to a low boil; this will take about 1 hour. As gray scum rises to the surface, skim it off continually.

When the water begins to boil, add the wine and continue to skim.

Add the salt, the clove-studded onion, the head of garlic, and the bouquet garni. Continue to skim until the liquid approaches a boil again. Cover with a lid slightly ajar and adjust the heat, repeatedly if necessary, so that a bare simmer is maintained. Cook for 2 hours. Check the pot from time to time; the liquid should never boil.

After 2 hours, add the carrots and the turnips and continue to simmer. Meanwhile, trim the stem ends from the leeks, remove and discard the dark green tops, and slit the white sections in half. Wash the leeks well and tie them together in a bundle. When the carrots and turnips have been cooking for 30 minutes, add the leeks to the pot and cook for 30 minutes more.

The pot-au-feu should be ready about 3 hours after it first comes to a boil. To test, pierce the beef shank with a sharp skewer to see if it is tender.

Skim the excess fat from the surface of the broth. Discard the onion, garlic and bouquet garni, and put the pig's foot aside for another use (such as in a salad). Remove the marrowbone from the wrapping and slip the marrow out onto a plate. Spread the marrow on the bread slices and place 1 slice in each of 6 shallow soup plates.

Ladle the broth directly from the pot into the soup plates, keeping the meats and vegetables in the broth so they stay hot. Snip the strings, carve the meats, and arrange them on a platter. Snip the string from the leeks and arrange the leeks and all the other vegetables around the meats. Serve the meats and vegetables as a separate course following the broth. Pour some broth into a small pitcher or bowl and place on the table for those who wish to moisten their meats. Offer the sea salt, capers, and olives at the table as well.

SERVES 6

Fried Meatballs

Polpette di Lesso

Tuscans—Florentines especially—are famously parsimonious and never waste food. Leftovers are always served again. These are not dreary, reheated dishes, but always transformed into something new, what the Italians refer to as *rifatti,* or remade. These meatballs are an example, and a good way of using leftover boiled or braised meat.

Salt

2 all-purpose or boiling potatoes

2 pounds boiled or roasted beef,
    chicken, or veal, or a combination

2 eggs

1 tablespoon chopped Italian parsley

1 tablespoon chopped fresh sage

1 clove garlic, peeled and finely
    chopped

1 teaspoon freshly grated lemon zest

Pinch freshly grated nutmeg

3 tablespoons freshly grated
    Parmigiano-Reggiano

Freshly ground pepper

⅔ cup fine dry breadcrumbs, home-
    made if possible

5 cups extra virgin olive oil for frying

Lemon wedges, optional

Bring a medium saucepan of water to a boil, and add a big pinch of salt and the potatoes. Boil the potatoes until tender, about 30 minutes. Drain the potatoes, refresh them under cold water and as soon as they are cool enough to handle, but still hot, peel and mash them.

Chop the meat very finely on a cutting board with a sharp chef's knife. Place the meat in a bowl and add the mashed potatoes, eggs, parsley, sage, garlic, lemon zest, nutmeg, and Parmigiano. Mix well and season well with salt and pepper.

With your hands, shape the mixture into ovals about 2½ inches long and 1 inch wide. Spread the breadcrumbs on a plate and coat the meatballs in them.

Heat the olive oil in a deep, heavy skillet to 350F on a deep-fat thermometer. If you do not have a thermometer, test the heat with a small piece of bread. Add the bread to the oil and if it is hot enough, bubbles will appear immediately around the bread and the cube will begin to brown.

Slip the meatballs, one by one, into the oil—do not crowd the pan. Fry the meatballs until golden brown all over, about 5 minutes. With a spatula or slotted spoon, remove them to a rack or to paper towels to drain in a warm spot. Arrange the meatballs on a platter, add the lemon wedges, and serve at once.

SERVES 6

Stuffed Beef Rolls

Bisteces Rellenos (Pajaritos)

In Mexico, these stuffed and rolled thin steaks are nicknamed *pajaritos*, or "little birds." The roasted tomato sauce has a rich, mildly spicy flavor.

2 pounds beef round or sirloin, cut into
   6 thin steaks
Salt
Freshly ground pepper
2 carrots, peeled and diced
1 pound fresh spinach, stems removed
10 thin slices baked or mild salt-cured
   ham, about 6 ounces total
5 ripe tomatoes, roasted (see Note)
2 cloves garlic, peeled and roasted
   (page 14)
¼ teaspoon ground cumin
⅛ teaspoon ground cloves
3 tablespoons vegetable or olive oil
¼ cup chopped onion
1 tablespoon flour
1½ cups homemade or good-quality
   unsalted commercial beef broth
½ cup dry red wine
2 bay leaves, fresh if possible
1 serrano chili, roughly chopped
2 tablespoons chopped fresh cilantro
   leaves

Cover each steak with a piece of wax paper or plastic wrap and pound until ¼ inch thick. Sprinkle lightly with salt and pepper and set aside.

Bring a small saucepan of water to a boil, add the carrots, and cook just until crisp-tender. Drain, refresh under cold water, and set aside in a small bowl. Wash the spinach well and place it in the saucepan with just the water clinging to its leaves. Cover and cook just to wilt. Drain and refresh, squeezing out excess water. Chop the spinach finely, add it to the carrots, and season it lightly with salt and pepper.

Place the slices of ham over the steaks, using more than one slice if necessary to cover. Divide the carrot-spinach mixture among the steaks, placing it along one long side. Starting with this side, roll the steaks up and tie them in two or three places with kitchen twine.

Puree the tomatoes, garlic, cumin, and cloves in a blender or food processor.

Heat the oil in a skillet, add the rolled steaks, and brown them lightly all over, 2 to 3 minutes. Transfer the rolls to a platter.

Add the onion to the skillet and sauté, for a minute or two, then add the flour and cook, stirring, for 2 minutes. Add the tomato-garlic puree and cook over high heat, stirring constantly, for 5 minutes. Add the broth, wine, bay leaves, and chili and simmer for 5 minutes. Correct the seasonings.

Return the rolled steaks along with any accumulated juices to the pan and cook over low heat, covered, for 10 minutes, or until the rolls are tender when pierced with the tip of a sharp knife. Snip and carefully remove the strings, place on a serving dish, sprinkle with the cilantro, and serve.

SERVES 6

NOTE To roast tomatoes, place them on a Mexican *comal* (see page 81), griddle, or cast-iron skillet over medium-high heat until the skin is charred. Alternatively, preheat the broiler and put the tomatoes on a foil-lined baking sheet and broil until the skin is charred, turning once.

Stuffed Meat Loaf with *Salsa de Jitomate*

Albondigón Relleno de Rajas

This specialty was presented at a Mexican culinary festival in 1975. The meat loaf is studded with red and green strips of chili, which become apparent when the loaf is sliced.

1 *bolillo* (hard bread roll), roughly cut
    up and soaked in milk
1 clove garlic, peeled
¼ onion
1 teaspoon dried oregano
1 teaspoon ground cumin
3 whole cloves
1 teaspoon salt
½ teaspoon freshly ground pepper
2½ pounds twice-ground lean beef
1 pound twice-ground pork
3 eggs
1 tablespoon dry breadcrumbs
3 poblano chilies, roasted, membranes
    removed, and cut into strips (page 14)
1 (6½-ounce) jar roasted red peppers,
    drained and cut into strips
8 ounces sliced bacon
Salsa de Jitomate (recipe follows)

Preheat the oven to 350°F. Drain the *bolillo*, tear it into small pieces and transfer it to a large bowl. In a *molcajete* (mortar and pestle) or food processor, grind together the garlic, onion, oregano, cumin, cloves, salt, and pepper. Transfer the mixture to the bowl with the bread and add the beef, pork, eggs, and breadcrumbs. Using your hands, combine the mixture thoroughly.

Transfer the meat mixture to a clean board and pat it into a rectangle about 10 inches long. Arrange the chilies and red pepper strips down the center. Roll the meat up lengthwise to form a loaf and place it in a baking pan or on a baking sheet. Lay the bacon slices over the top of the loaf. Bake for about 1 hour, or until the juices run clear.

Serve the meat loaf with the *salsa de jitomate,* warm or at room temperature.

SERVES 6 TO 8

Salsa de Jitomate

2½ pounds fresh ripe tomatoes, peeled
   and cut into chunks

1 clove garlic, peeled

¼ onion

¼ teaspoon dried thyme

¼ teaspoon ground cumin

1 whole clove

1 tablespoon butter

1 teaspoon salt

¼ teaspoon freshly ground pepper

In a blender or food processor, puree the tomatoes, garlic, onion, thyme, cumin, and clove with ¼ cup water. Melt the butter in a small skillet, add the tomato puree, the salt, and pepper and bring to a boil. Boil for 5 minutes, then lower the heat and cook at a low simmer, uncovered, for 10 minutes longer.

Ground Beef Salad

Laab Nuea

This popular dish found its way to Bangkok thanks to the people of the northeastern region of Thailand. The fresh herbs and lime juice make it a refreshing salad; chicken or pork can be used in place of the beef. Serve this with raw vegetables such as long beans, finely sliced cabbage, spinach, or basil leaves. Galangal powder can be found in Thai or other Asian markets and even in other well-stocked specialty markets.

1 pound coarsely ground or minced beef
¼ cup fresh lime juice
2 tablespoons *nam pla* (Thai fish sauce)
½ teaspoon galangal powder (*kha pon*)
6 shallots, thinly sliced
2 tablespoons chopped green onion

2 tablespoons chopped cilantro leaves
2 tablespoons ground roasted sticky rice
  (see Note)
1 teaspoon ground red Thai chili pepper,
  optional
15 mint leaves for garnish

Combine the ground or minced beef with the lime juice, *nam pla,* galangal powder, and shallots.

Place a skillet over medium heat, add the beef mixture, and cook, stirring, for five minutes, or until the beef is just cooked (no longer raw).

Remove the skillet from the heat and add the chopped green onion and cilantro and the ground, roasted rice. Mix thoroughly to combine well. Transfer the mixture to a serving plate, spoon the ground red pepper, if using, on the side, and garnish with mint leaves.

SERVES 2 TO 4

NOTE To make roasted sticky rice, place raw sticky rice on a hot skillet and cook it, stirring, until it is golden brown. Add a tablespoon of water from time to time. Once cooled, the rice can be ground in a small food processor or spice or coffee grinder and kept in a jar.

Waterfall Beef

Nuea Yang Nam Tok

The name is perhaps a touch over-the-top in poetic terms—inspired as it is by the sound of the dripping juices of the steak cooking over the charcoal fire—but it does justice to this tasty dish.

1 pound boneless sirloin steak

⅓ cup *nam pla* (Thai fish sauce)

¼ cup fresh lime juice

2 tablespoons chopped scallions

2 tablespoons chopped cilantro leaves

¼ cup mint leaves

1½ tablespoons ground roasted sticky
    rice (opposite page)

1 tablespoon toasted sesame seeds

½ teaspoon ground chili pepper (*prik
    khee noo pon*)

Raw or blanched vegetables: beans,
    lettuces, spinach, or basil leaves

Prepare a charcoal fire. Place the steak in a dish, rub both sides with 1 tablespoon of fish sauce, and set aside to marinate for 5 minutes. When the fire is ready, grill the steak for 3 minutes on each side, or to medium-rare. Remove the steak to a cutting board and let it rest for 2 minutes, then slice it into pieces ⅛ inch thick by about 1 by 2 inches.

Place the pieces of steak in a medium saucepan and add the remaining fish sauce and the lime juice. Place the pan over medium-high heat and stir for about 1 minute. Remove from the heat and add the scallions, cilantro, mint, ground roasted rice, sesame seeds, and ground chili pepper; stir to combine thoroughly.

Place the beef mixture on a serving plate with a selection of raw or blanched vegetables.

SERVES 4

Korean Barbecue

Bulgogi

The Korean words for this dish—*bulgogi* or *bulgalbi,* grilled strips and ribs of beef—describe a very old tradition of cooking on a curved iron hotplate. The modern Korean barbecue takes place on cone-shaped hotplates fitted over tabletop burners. All sorts of meats, including mutton, pork, and poultry, innards, and seafood are cooked this way, after being well marinated in a spicy, deeply flavored mixture. The cooking itself is swift, just enough to sear the surface and cook through the meat. Serve Korean barbecue with white rice and Yangnyum Kanjang sauce and other typical accompaniments, like *kim chee* (pickled cabbage).

2 pounds lean beef tenderloin or filet
½ cup light soy sauce
¼ cup dark soy sauce
3 tablespoons finely chopped scallions
2 to 3 teaspoons minced garlic
½ teaspoon freshly ground pepper
1 tablespoon sugar
2 tablespoons sesame seeds, toasted
  and ground
1 tablespoon dark (Asian) sesame oil
Yangnyum Kanjang (recipe follows)

Cut the beef across the grain into very thin slices, then into strips about 2 inches wide. Whisk the remaining ingredients together in a medium glass dish or stainless steel dish with ½ cup water. Add the beef and stir thoroughly. Cover and marinate at cool room temperature or in the refrigerator for at least 3 hours. When ready to serve, remove the meat from the marinade and arrange it on a serving platter or 6 individual plates.

Preheat a tabletop broiler, protecting the table with an asbestos mat or other heat shield. Using chopsticks or small fondue forks, cook the meat quickly on both sides on the broiler, then dip it into the sauce before eating.

SERVES 6

Yangnyum Kanjang

The sauce can be prepared a day in advance and stored in a covered container in the refrigerator.

¼ cup light soy sauce
1 tablespoon rice wine or Chinese brown vinegar or rice vinegar
1 tablespoon finely chopped scallion
½ teaspoon minced garlic

½ to 1½ teaspoon hot chili sauce, or to taste
1½ teaspoons sesame seeds, toasted and ground

Mix all the ingredients together with 1½ to 2 tablespoons water in a small bowl. Divide the sauce among several small dishes for serving.

Best-of-the-Border Barbecue Brisket

This is a dish typical of today's Texas cooking, which developed out of the style established by the cowboys and traders who came to the Southwest in great numbers in the nineteenth century. Their chuckwagon chow often featured meat cooked over mesquite fires. This dish also reflects the dry-rub marinade school, whose devotees insist is the only correct and authentically Texan way to barbecue brisket. Needless to say, the wet marinade group feels just as strongly.

Whichever marinade is used, the results are also dependent on the cooking method and the way of regulating the heat, which are rather elaborate. To duplicate them, you will need to place a metal pan half filled with water beneath the cooking rack of your grill, and bank your coals, along with presoaked wood chips, along the sides. Finally, it is important to maintain a low heat level so that the meat cooks slowly. This is not so complicated as it sounds, and the results are well worth the effort.

9 to 10 pounds beef brisket

FOR THE DRY RUB
¾ cup kosher or sea salt
½ cup freshly ground pepper
⅓ cup chili powder
4½ teaspoons cayenne pepper

¼ to ⅓ cup dark beer

FOR THE BARBECUE SAUCE
¼ cup bacon drippings or butter
1 yellow onion, peeled and coarsely
  chopped

1 cup ketchup
2 tablespoons Worcestershire
  sauce
¼ cup red wine vinegar
1 cup dark beer
2 tablespoons chili powder
1 tablespoon dry mustard
1 teaspoon salt
1 teaspoon freshly ground pepper
½ teaspoon cayenne pepper or 2 pickled
  jalapeño peppers, minced
2 cloves garlic, peeled and minced

Prepare an indirect-heat fire in a kettle-style charcoal grill or other covered grill and oil the grill rack (make your fire and prepare the grill according to the headnote).

Remove the fat from the side of the large end of the brisket.

To make the dry rub: Combine all the ingredients in a small bowl. Rub the mixture generously all over the brisket and place it, fat side up, on the grill rack. Pack any remaining dry rub on top. Place a thermometer in the grill, cover it, and cook the brisket at 250 to 275°F for 4 hours, adding charcoal and wood chips as needed.

Remove the brisket from the grill. Using heavy-duty foil, make a pouch large enough to accommodate the brisket, pinching it together on three sides. Place the brisket into the pouch and add the beer. Seal the open side closed.

Return the brisket in its pouch to the grill rack. Increase the amount of fuel in order to raise the temperature to about 300°F. Continue to cook for another 3 hours, letting the temperature drop back down to 225 to 250°F.

As the brisket cooks, make the barbecue sauce: Combine all of the sauce ingredients in a medium saucepan, bring just to a boil, and stir to combine well. Reduce the heat to medium and simmer the sauce, uncovered, until thickened, 20 to 25 minutes.

Remove the brisket from the pouch, slice the meat against the grain, and arrange it on a platter. Pass the warm barbecue sauce at the table.

SERVES 10 TO 12

Braised Veal Shanks with Lemon

Ossobuchi al Limone

This is a variation on the more familiar classic veal shanks with *gremolata,* the aromatic mixture of lemon and parsley and sometimes, garlic. In this somewhat lighter version, the flavorful lemon and parsley are incorporated into the sauce. Fresh *tagliatelle*—thin, flat pasta—lightly dressed with butter and freshly ground Parmigiano-Reggiano cheese are delightful on the side.

6 pieces veal shank, each about 7
    ounces and 1 inch thick
1 cup flour
Salt
Freshly ground pepper
3 tablespoons unsalted butter
3 tablespoons extra virgin olive oil
1 recipe homemade or good-quality
    commercial veal broth, light beef
    broth, or chicken broth
2 tablespoons chopped Italian parsley
Juice of 2 lemons

Make several cuts in the edges of the veal pieces so that they will not curl while cooking. Combine the flour with salt and pepper to taste on a plate or sheet of waxed paper. Dredge the veal pieces well in the flour mixture, shaking off the excess.

Meanwhile, place a large, heavy skillet over medium-high heat and add the butter and oil. When the butter stops foaming, add the pieces of veal and brown well on both sides, about 10 minutes total. (Try to have the pan ready to receive the veal as soon as the shanks are floured, so that they will not absorb the flour and will brown nicely.)

Add about ¼ cup of the broth to the skillet, season to taste with salt and pepper, cover, and simmer over very low heat, about 1 hour, adding additional broth as needed to keep the meat moist. Turn the meat once while it is cooking. The meat should be fork tender but not falling apart.

When the veal is ready, add the parsley and the lemon juice to the pan. Turn the veal pieces to pick up the seasonings, cover, and cook for 5 minutes longer. Transfer the veal shanks to a warmed platter, spoon the cooking juices over, and serve.

SERVES 6

Braised Veal Shank with Herbs

Stinco alle Erbe

While the cut pieces of the veal shank are now familiar as *osso buco,* and easily available to American home cooks, the whole shank, called the *stinco* in Italian, is less familiar. You may need to order it in advance from your butcher, or from a market that has a good meat department. It is worth the effort, as is finding and using fresh herbs for this preparation. If you cannot find fresh bay leaves, thyme, or marjoram, dried will be aromatic enough and can be substituted, but dry sage should be avoided.

1 tablespoon unsalted butter

3 tablespoons extra virgin olive oil

1 whole veal shank (shin), about
   3½ pounds

Salt

Freshly ground pepper

3 fresh bay leaves

3 fresh sage leaves

5 juniper berries

1 tablespoon chopped fresh thyme, or
   1 teaspoon dried

1 tablespoon chopped fresh marjoram,
   or 1 teaspoon dried

1 fresh rosemary sprig

¼ cup cognac or other good-quality
   brandy

1 cup homemade or good-quality
   commercial veal broth or light beef
   broth

Preheat the oven to 350°F.

In a large, deep, heavy ovenproof pot, melt the butter with the oil over medium heat. Add the veal shank and brown it well on all sides, turning it frequently, about 15 minutes. Season to taste with salt and pepper. Pierce the meat with a large fork to help allow the marrow to escape during cooking and flavor the juices.

Add the bay leaves, sage leaves, juniper berries, thyme, marjoram, rosemary, and cognac. Raise the heat to high and allow the liquor to evaporate. Add the broth and cover the pot.

Place the pot in the oven and cook, turning the veal occasionally in its cooking juices, until very tender, about 3 hours.

Transfer the veal to a warmed platter to rest for about 10 minutes, then serve. The meat will be quite soft, and can be easily cut away from the bone. Bits of marrow can be added to each serving with some of the cooking juices.

SERVES 4

Veal Stew with Mushrooms and Peas

Historically, in the United States veal was much more popular in the South and Midwest than it was in other parts of the country. For a time veal also was very inexpensive, cheap enough that nearly ten times as much was consumed in the 1930s and 1940s than is consumed today. This stew is from Savannah; steamed potatoes, buttered noodles, or rice are good with it.

5 tablespoons unsalted butter

3 pounds stewing veal, cut into 1-inch cubes

1½ tablespoons flour

Salt

Freshly ground pepper

1 medium onion, finely chopped

½ cup homemade or good-quality chicken broth

½ cup dry white wine

An herb bouquet of 1 thyme sprig, 3 sprigs parsley, 1 bay leaf, 1 scallion, and 1 crushed garlic clove, tied together in cheesecloth

2 teaspoons vegetable oil

½ pound wild, cultivated, or mixed mushroom caps

½ cup shelled green peas

2 egg yolks

¼ cup heavy cream

⅛ teaspoon freshly grated nutmeg

Dash hot red pepper sauce

1 tablespoon lemon juice

Chopped fresh Italian parsley for garnish

Place a large, heavy saucepan or casserole over medium heat, and add 4 tablespoons of butter to melt. Dry the veal with paper towels, then add it to the pan, in batches if necessary to avoid crowding, and brown it evenly. Sprinkle with the flour and season to taste with salt and pepper. Add the onion and cook, stirring, for 2 minutes. Stir in the broth and wine and bring just to the boil. Add the herb bouquet, lower the heat, and cover. Cook over medium-low heat until the meat is tender, about 50 minutes, stirring occasionally.

Meanwhile, heat the remaining butter with the oil in a large skillet over medium-high heat. Add the mushroom caps and sauté until golden. Set aside.

When the veal is tender, discard the herb bouquet and add the mushrooms and peas to the pan. Cook, uncovered, for 5 minutes. Reduce the heat to low.

In a small bowl, beat the egg yolks with the cream. Remove about 2 tablespoons of liquid from the stew and very slowly whisk it into the egg mixture. When the liquid has been incorporated, stir the mixture into the stew. Taking care to keep the heat very low, heat until the sauce thickens just enough to coat a spoon, about 3 minutes. Take care not to let the liquid boil or the eggs will curdle. Add the nutmeg, hot pepper sauce, lemon juice and, if necessary, additional salt and pepper to taste. Sprinkle with the parsley and serve.

SERVES 6

Calf's Liver and Bacon with Orange-Leek Sauce

L amb or venison liver may also be used in this dish. The important thing in any liver preparation is to buy it the day you plan to use it. Fresh is best. This is good with fluffy mashed potatoes and a green vegetable or grilled sweet onions.

8 slices bacon

1 teaspoon unsalted butter

1 leek, white part only, washed, thinly sliced, and drained well

¼ cup flour

Salt

Freshly ground pepper

4 thin slices calf's liver, about 1 pound total

Zest of ½ orange

Juice of ½ orange (about ¼ cup)

Place the bacon in a large, heavy skillet and fry until crisp; transfer to paper towels or a baking rack to drain. Pour off all but 1 tablespoon of the fat and set the skillet aside.

Place a separate small skillet over medium heat, add the butter, and melt it. Add the leek, lower the heat, cover, and cook slowly until tender, about 10 minutes. Set aside.

Return the large skillet with the bacon fat to the stovetop over medium-high heat. Season the flour with salt and pepper to taste and spread it on a plate or a sheet of waxed paper. Dredge the liver slices in the seasoned flour and shake off the excess. Place the slices in the hot fat and sauté for 1 to 2 minutes on each side for medium-rare, or longer to taste. Transfer the slices to a serving platter and keep warm.

Raise the heat to high under the leeks. Add the orange zest and juice and bring to a boil, stirring for a minute or so. Season the sauce lightly with salt and pepper. Remove and discard the zest and pour the orange-leek sauce over the liver. Arrange the bacon to the side of the liver slices and serve.

SERVES 4

Harvesters' Calf's Liver

Foie de Veau à la Moissonneuse

This French dish is often made with lamb's liver and is essentially the same as the well-known Venetian specialty *fegato alla veneziana*. This version is said to have been a great favorite of the wheat harvesters in the Vaucluse region of France in the last century.

5 tablespoons olive oil
1 pound large sweet onions, halved and sliced paper thin (you can do this in a food processor using the thin-slicing attachment)
1 fresh bay leaf
1 sprig fresh thyme
3 cloves garlic, peeled and finely chopped
6 tablespoons finely chopped Italian parsley
Salt
½ cup dry red wine
¾ pound calf's liver, in one piece
Freshly ground pepper
Flour
2 tablespoons red wine vinegar

Warm 2 tablespoons of the olive oil in a large, flameproof earthenware casserole or heavy sauté pan over very low heat. Add the onions, bay leaf, thyme, garlic, parsley, and salt to taste. Cover and allow the onions to sweat, stirring a couple of times, for about 45 minutes. The onions should cook and soften completely in their own juices, but not take on color.

Remove the lid, turn up the heat slightly, and allow the onions to color very slightly—just lightly golden brown; stir from time to time. Add the wine, bring just to a boil, then lower the heat, and simmer over low heat, uncovered, until the mixture is reduced to the consistency of a sauce, about 15 minutes. Remove and discard the thyme sprig and bay leaf. Add a generous amount of pepper.

Meanwhile, cut the liver into thin slices, about ½ inch thick, then cut each slice into 1-inch pieces. Season the pieces with salt and pepper. Dredge the liver in the flour, shaking off the excess; it is effective to shake them in a sieve to do this.

Warm the remaining 3 tablespoons olive oil in a large sauté pan. Add the liver squares and sauté them quickly, tossing and stirring, until slightly firmed up but still rare, not more than a minute or two.

Transfer the liver to the onion sauce. Raise the heat under the sauté pan in which the liver was cooked and pour in the vinegar. Quickly deglaze the pan, scraping the bottom to dissolve all the browned bits. Add these juices to the liver and onion mixture and serve at once.

SERVES 4

Venison Stew with Prunes

S tewing or braising venison brings out its full rich flavor. This savory stew is delicious with soft polenta. The return of venison to the national table, along with our casual acquaintance with the various ingredients of this dish, typify the new American cooking.

2 pounds boneless venison rump or
  shoulder, trimmed of excess fat and
  connective tissue, cut into 1-inch
  cubes
1 tablespoon juniper berries, crushed
1 tablespoon whole black peppercorns
2 cloves garlic, peeled and coarsely
  chopped
1½ cups dry red wine
2 to 3 tablespoons olive oil
2 cups cleaned, trimmed celery, cut on
  the diagonal into 1-inch pieces
6 to 8 small boiling onions, peeled
½ pound pitted prunes
¾ to 1 cup homemade or best-quality
  commercial beef broth
Salt
Freshly ground pepper

Place the venison, juniper berries, pepper-corns, garlic, and 1 cup of the wine in a large glass bowl or ceramic or stainless steel bowl. Stir to combine, cover, and let marinate in the refrigerator for 2 to 3 hours or overnight.

Preheat the oven to 350°F.

Drain the venison and discard the mari-nade. Pat the meat dry with paper towels. Heat the olive oil in a large, heavy, oven-proof skillet over high heat. Add the veni-son cubes, in batches if necessary to avoid crowding, and brown them well all over. Add the celery, onions, and prunes. Add the remaining ½ cup wine and ¾ cup of the broth. Season to taste with salt and pepper. Bring the liquid just to a simmer, cover the pan, and place in the oven. Braise the venison for 45 minutes, or until tender, adding the remaining stock if nec-essary and adjusting the heat to keep the liquid just at a simmer. Adjust the season-ings with salt and pepper to taste.

SERVES 4 TO 6

Marinated Buffalo Steak

Buffalo—or, more accurately, American bison—can be substituted in almost any recipe for beef. Buffalo is lower in fat and cholesterol and generally has a sweeter flavor than beef. Because of bison's lower fat content, its meat is darker and should be cooked only to rare to medium over low heat and for shorter cooking times than beef. Farm-raised American bison is available from butchers and specialty grocers and by mail order, in cuts similar to those of beef. Grilled vegetables and a tomato or hot-pepper salsa would be good with this.

1 small head garlic

½ cup olive oil

¼ cup orange juice

1 tablespoon grated orange zest

½ cup dry red wine

¼ cup chopped red onion

1 tablespoon balsamic vinegar

2 tablespoons raspberry vinegar

Salt

1 teaspoon freshly ground pepper

5 juniper berries, crushed

1 bay leaf, crumbled

1 sprig rosemary

1 tablespoon chopped fresh tarragon

1 tablespoon chopped fresh sage

1 buffalo sirloin steak, about 2 pounds and about 2 inches thick

Preheat the oven to 350°F. Brush the head of garlic liberally all over with the olive oil, wrap it in heavy-duty aluminum foil, and place it in the oven to roast for about 1 hour. When the garlic is soft when pierced with a cake tester or toothpick, remove it from the oven.

Combine the roasted garlic flesh with all the remaining ingredients, with the exception of the buffalo steak, in a shallow glass dish or stainless steel dish. Add the buffalo steak to the marinade, turn to coat evenly, cover, and refrigerate overnight, turning several times.

Remove the steak from the refrigerator 30 minutes before cooking. Prepare a charcoal fire or preheat the broiler. Cook the steak for 5 to 6 minutes on each side for medium-rare. Let the steak rest for a few minutes before slicing and serving.

SERVES 6

Buffalo Filet with Peppercorns and Mustard

The filet can be cooked over charcoal, in which case it should not be trimmed of all its fat, so that it self-bastes and keeps the fire lively. The meat can also be spit-roasted, either in a conventional oven or over a wood or charcoal fire.

1 buffalo filet, about 4 pounds, partially trimmed of fat

3 large cloves garlic, peeled and cut into slivers

6 tablespoons smooth or whole-grain Dijon mustard

3 tablespoons cracked peppercorns

Preheat the oven to 375°F. Using the point of a small sharp knife, make slits about ½ inch deep all over the filet. Push the garlic slivers into the slits, then spread the mustard all over the filet. Roll the filet in the peppercorns, pressing them into the mustard.

Place the filet in a roasting pan and place the dish in the oven. Roast, turning from time to time, to brown evenly, 20 to 25 minutes for medium-rare.

Remove the filet to a cutting board and let it rest for a few minutes before slicing. Place the slices on a warmed platter and serve.

SERVES 8 TO 10

TWO

Pork

Pork with Rosemary

Arista di Maiale al Rosmarino

This is a typical Tuscan preparation, very, very simple and perfectly delicious. You can tuck another sprig or two of rosemary between the bones and the meat. You'll need a center-cut loin of pork on the bone; ask your butcher to separate but not completely remove the chine bone underneath the roast. The roast will be more flavorful and the carving will be easy.

1 or more sprigs fresh rosemary

6 cloves garlic, crushed and peeled

Salt

Freshly ground pepper

1 loin of pork, about 2½ pounds, with bones (see Headnote)

2 tablespoons extra virgin olive oil

1 tablespoon unsalted butter, at room temperature

½ cup dry white wine

Preheat the oven to 400°F.

Remove the rosemary leaves from the sprigs and chop the leaves. Mix the rosemary and garlic with salt to taste and a generous amount of pepper. Rub this mixture all over the meat. Tie the roast securely to the chine with kitchen twine. Place the roast in a heavy baking pan, roasting pan, or cast-iron skillet. Rub with the oil and butter. Roast for about 1½ hours, turning and basting several times. When done, the meat should be nicely browned and cooked through, but not dry.

Remove the twine, separate the meat from the chine bone, and let the meat rest in a warm spot. With a spoon, carefully remove some of the excess fat from the roasting pan, then place the pan on the stovetop over medium-high heat. Pour in the wine, scraping up any browned bits from the bottom of the pan. Season to taste. Cut the pork into thick slices, arrange on a serving platter, and serve with the pan sauce. The meat can be cut entirely away from the rib bones before carving, or these bones can be served with the slices.

SERVES 4 TO 6

Roast Pork with Olives and Anchovies

Rôti de Porc à la Toulonnaise

In Provence, sage is the herb of choice for pork. Olives and anchovies are among the region's other favored ingredients. Do not try this with dried sage, which has an off-putting, musty flavor. As with all simple dishes, God is in the details: Do not use canned olives. Any good black olive, easily found at specialty food markets, will do: niçoise, Gaeta, Sicilian, or various Middle Eastern types.

Ask your butcher to cut along the tenderloin to separate it from the rest of the roast, without cutting all the way through the piece. Or do this yourself with a sharp boning knife.

2 tablespoons finely minced parsley
1 clove garlic, peeled and finely minced
A 3-pound boned pork loin, with the
    tenderloin separated but still
    attached
Salt
Freshly ground pepper
8 anchovies, packed in salt, rinsed,
    patted dry, and filleted
⅔ cup black olives, pitted and chopped
    (see Headnote)
Several fresh sage sprigs
½ cup dry white wine

Preheat the oven to 450°F.

Combine the parsley and garlic and chop together; the mixture, known as a *persil-*

lade, should be very fine. Place the pork roast on a work surface, with the back side down. Sprinkle with salt and pepper, then with the *persillade.* Distribute the anchovies and olives along the tenderloin section of the roast. Roll up the loin and tie it with kitchen twine. Slash the fat side with a sharp knife. Insert whole small sprigs of the sage or larger leaves into the slits. Place the roast into a roasting pan.

Put the pan in the oven and roast for 10 minutes. Reduce the heat to 325°F. After 30 minutes, begin basting regularly with the pan juices. After 45 minutes, remove most of the fat from the pan, add a few spoonfuls of the wine, and continue basting every 3 to 4 minutes; add more wine as needed if it evaporates. The roast should be completely cooked and nicely glazed after about 1¼ hours.

Remove the roast to a cutting board, snip off the twine, and cut the roast into slices about ⅓ inch thick. Lay the slices, overlapping, on a warm serving platter. Pour the juices from the pan, along with any from carving, over the slices and serve at once.

Serves 6

Pork Tenderloin with Cranberry-Chipotle Sauce

Chipotle chilies are smoke-dried jalapeños. For this recipe, you want the variety that comes canned in red adobo sauce. You may need to go to a specialty market, but a supermarket with a reasonably good section devoted to Mexican ingredients should have it. Frozen cranberries can be substituted if fresh ones are out of season. Thanks to the popularity of Southwestern cooking, which exploded in the 1980s, the flavor of chilies has insinuated itself into regional styles from coast to coast.

FOR THE PORK
1½ pounds pork tenderloin
Salt
Freshly ground pepper
1 tablespoon unsalted butter
1 tablespoon olive oil

FOR THE SAUCE
2 tablespoons minced shallots
2 cloves garlic, peeled and minced
2 cups cranberries

3 tablespoons sugar
1 cup dry red wine
2½ cups homemade or good-quality
    store-bought chicken broth
1 canned chipotle chili in adobo sauce,
    pureed
1 teaspoon minced fresh sage
3 tablespoons unsalted butter, at room
    temperature
Salt
Freshly ground pepper

Preheat the oven to 375°F.

Wipe the pork all over with paper towels and season it well with salt and freshly ground pepper. Place a skillet large enough to hold the pork over medium-high heat; add the butter and oil. When the butter stops foaming, place the pork in the pan, and brown it all over. Transfer the meat to a rack in a baking pan and place the pan in the oven. Roast the pork until an instant-read thermometer reaches 150F, about 40 minutes; the meat should retain some pink at the center—do not let it overcook. Reserve the drippings in the skillet.

Meanwhile, make the sauce. Sauté the shallots and garlic in the reserved drippings in the skillet for about 30 seconds. Add the cranberries and sugar and cook, stirring, for 30 seconds. Add the red wine, scraping up any browned bits from the pan. Raise the heat to high and boil the mixture to reduce it to about ¾ cup, 10 to 15 minutes. Add the chicken broth, chipotle puree, and sage. Boil the mixture until it is reduced to about 2 cups, about 10 minutes. Strain the sauce into a saucepan and bring to a simmer. Whisk in the butter in bits and season with salt and pepper to taste. Remove the sauce to a warm spot.

When the pork is done, remove it from the oven, cover it loosely with aluminum foil, and let it rest for 10 minutes. Place the meat on a cutting board and cut it into ½-inch slices. Divide the slices among 6 dinner plates and spoon sauce over them. Serve immediately.

SERVES 6

Roast Leg of Pork in Adobo Sauce

Pierna de Cerdo Adobada

This dish is perfect for a festive buffet and easy to prepare in advance. The marinade can be doubled and served as a sauce. Almost any of your favorite Mexican or Southwestern American side dishes would be perfect to complete the meal.

2 cups freshly squeezed orange juice
6 ancho chilies, seeds and membranes removed
8 pasilla chilies, seeds and membranes removed
¼ medium onion, coarsely chopped
⅓ cup cider vinegar
10 cloves garlic, peeled
1 teaspoon dried thyme
3 whole cloves
1 teaspoon ground cumin
1 tablespoon dried oregano
One 2-inch stick cinnamon
3 whole allspice
2 tablespoons coarse salt
1 leg of pork (fresh ham; see Notes), about 9 pounds
2 tablespoons lard

In a small saucepan heat 1 cup of the orange juice until just warm. Toast the chilies on a Mexican *comal* (see Notes) or in a cast-iron skillet, then place them in the orange juice to soak for 20 minutes. Transfer the juice and chilies to a blender or food processor, add the onion and vinegar, and process.

In a mortar or small electric grinder, grind the garlic, thyme, cloves, cumin, oregano, cinnamon stick, allspice, and salt. Add the pureed chili mixture and stir to combine. Add enough of the remaining orange juice until the mixture has the consistency of yogurt.

Using a fork, pierce the leg of pork all over. Transfer the meat to a baking pan or dish, spread the chili-orange mixture all over it, and refrigerate for at least 6 hours, preferably 24 hours. Turn the roast several times while it is marinating.

Two hours before roasting, remove the leg of pork from the refrigerator, spread the lard lightly and evenly all over, and set aside.

Preheat the oven to 350°F. Cover the leg of pork loosely with heavy-duty aluminum foil, place the pan in the oven, and roast for 2 hours, basting from time to time with the pan juices. Turn the meat and roast for another hour, or until the meat can easily be pierced with a fork. Turn the meat again, if necessary, to place it fat side up. Raise the heat to 450F, remove the foil, and roast the pork until nicely browned, taking care not to let it burn, 10 to 15 min-utes. Let the meat rest for 15 minutes before carving.

SERVES 12 TO 16

NOTE You may want to order the leg of pork in advance to be sure you will have it, as some markets do not always stock whole ones.

NOTE A *comal* is a simple and endlessly useful Mexican cooking utensil, a thin unglazed clay or metal circular plate that is placed over heat to cook tortillas or to roast tomatoes, garlic, or onions. *Comals* are widely available.

Sweet and Savory Pork Leg with Rice

Khao Ka Moo

The delicious sauce that flavors this pork as it cooks can also be used for braising other meats.

1 cup light soy sauce

½ cup sweet soy sauce

¼ cup Maggi brand seasoning

¼ cup brown sugar

1 teaspoon salt

6 cloves garlic, peeled and minced

1 teaspoon freshly ground white
  pepper

¼ cup fresh cilantro leaves

⅛ teaspoon ground cardamom

⅛ teaspoon ground cinnamon

4 whole star anise

1 piece leg of pork or picnic ham, about
  2 pounds, from the chump end

½ cup fresh cilantro leaves for garnish

4 cups cooked hot jasmine or short-
  grained rice

Combine all of the ingredients up to the pork with 1 cup water in a deep pot or Dutch oven that can accommodate the pork. Bring just to a boil, stirring to combine and to dissolve the sugar. Add the leg of pork. Cover and simmer over low heat, turning the pork 2 or 3 times while it cooks, for 1 hour, or until tender.

When the pork is cooked, remove it from the pot, cut it into thin slices, and arrange on a platter. Garnish with the cilantro leaves. Strain the sauce into a serving bowl and serve it with the pork and the cooked rice.

SERVES 6 TO 8

Catalonian Pork Brochettes

Pincho Moruno

These spicy pork morsels can be found at tapas bars all over Spain. *Pincho Moruno* translates to "Moorish mouthful," which hints at this recipe's origin. In Arab countries, of course, pork is not prepared; lamb is used for such kebabs. In Spain, however, pork has become the meat of choice. If you wish to use this recipe for tapas, cut the meat into 1-inch cubes; this will yield 8 servings. The marinade can also be rubbed on a boneless pork loin, which can then be roasted or grilled.

2 pounds pork, cut into 1½-inch cubes
½ cup olive oil
1 tablespoon paprika
2 tablespoons ground cumin
1 teaspoon chopped fresh thyme
2 teaspoons cayenne pepper
1 tablespoon fresh oregano, or
   1 teaspoon dried
2 teaspoons minced fresh garlic

Place the pork in a glass bowl or other nonreactive container.

Place a small skillet over low heat. Add the oil, then all of the remaining ingredients. Warm gently, without browning, for about 1 minute; remove from the heat and cool to room temperature. Rub the herb and spice mixture evenly over the pork, cover, and refrigerate overnight.

When ready to cook, allow the meat to return to room temperature. Meanwhile, prepare a charcoal fire or preheat the broiler.

Divide the pork cubes among 4 metal skewers and place them over the fire or on the broiler pan. Cook, turning once, until done to taste, about 4 minutes per side for medium-rare, 5 minutes for medium. Take care not to overcook. Transfer to a warmed platter and serve.

SERVES 4

Skewered Pork Roasted with Malt Sugar

The malt sugar, which is made into a syrup that is brushed over the pork as it roasts, produces a rich, red-brown glaze, a crisp texture, and a sweet flavor. Somewhat fatty pork should be used for this dish or the skin will burn and the flesh become dry during cooking. The Fen liquor called for is a strong spirit used mainly in marinades. You may find it in a well-stocked Chinatown market, but the substitutes listed will give fine results.

1 pound pork leg, with some fat

1½ tablespoons light soy sauce

1 tablespoon dark or mushroom soy sauce

1 tablespoon Fen liquor, rice wine, or dry sherry

2 tablespoons soybean oil

¼ teaspoon salt

1 tablespoon sugar

1 teaspoon dark (Asian) sesame oil

3 tablespoons malt sugar or brown sugar

Cut the pork into thin strips and place in a glass dish or other nonreactive container. Combine all of the remaining ingredients with the exception of the malt sugar and pour over the pork. Stir, cover, and place in a cool spot or in the refrigerator to marinate for 2 to 3 hours, turning from time to time.

Preheat the oven to 400°F.

Remove the pork from the marinade, letting the excess drip off but do not pat dry. Thread the pieces of pork onto one or more thick metal skewers and suspend them from a rack in the oven over a drip pan for 10 minutes.

Meanwhile, bring ½ cup water to a boil and mix it with the malt sugar, stirring until dissolved. Remove the pork from the oven and brush it liberally with the syrup, return it to the oven, and roast for 5 minutes more. Remove, brush again with the syrup, and roast for about another minute. Remove the pork from the oven and give it a final brushing with the syrup.

If the strips are very long, cut them into 2- to 3-inch pieces and arrange on a serving plate. Serve warm or at room temperature.

SERVES 2 TO 4

Meat Uruapan Style

Carnitas Estilo Uruapan

In the Mexican city of Uruapan, large shallow copper pots from nearby Santa Clara del Cobre are used to cook these "little meats," which are always served with tortillas and salsa so that each person can fashion his own tacos. Serve with hot corn tortillas and guacamole and/or tomato salsa.

2 pounds boneless pork, with some fat,
    cut into 2-inch chunks
¼ onion
2 cloves garlic, peeled
1 tablespoon salt
1 tablespoon lard
½ cup freshly squeezed orange juice
½ cup milk

Place the pork, onion, garlic, and salt and 8 cups water in a large, heavy pot or Dutch oven. Bring to a boil, cover, and cook over medium heat for 1½ hours, or until the pork is very tender. Drain the meat in a colander.

Melt the lard in a saucepan. As soon as it bubbles, add the orange juice and milk, then the pork. Cook, uncovered, over medium heat until the meat is browned, 15 to 20 minutes. (The orange juice and milk will cook off, leaving the pork to brown.) Stir from time to time and adjust the heat as needed to prevent burning. Drain the meat immediately in a colander to eliminate all the excess fat. Serve with warm tortillas and salsa.

SERVES 6

Pork Curry

Gaeng Moo Tay Po

This dish is familiar in Bangkok and the Central Plains of Thailand. Curries are popular throughout the country and are most often made with chicken, beef, or seafood. This is the usual base for a pork curry and is quite simple to assemble once the Thai ingredients are in hand; they can be found in Asian markets and even some well-stocked supermarkets.

3 cups unsweetened coconut milk

3 tablespoons red curry paste (*nam prik gaeng ped*)

1 pound pork, cut into 1-inch cubes

¼ cup Thai fish sauce (*nam pla*)

2 tablespoons sugar

¼ cup tamarind juice (*ma-kaam piag*)

8 whole Kaffir lime leaves (*bai ma-grood*)

4 cups swamp cabbage or spinach, cut into 1-inch pieces

Combine one third of the coconut milk with the curry paste in a large saucepan and heat for 1 minute.

Add the pork, bring just to a very low simmer, and cook until the pork is tender, about 30 minutes. Add the remaining ingredients, and bring just to a low boil. Serve with hot rice.

SERVES 4

Pork Cutlets with Tapenade

Escalopes de Porc à la Tapenade

Tapeno is the Provençal word for capers, the key ingredient in the spread that is as versatile as it is ubiquitous in the South of France. The recipe here is a more or less basic version—others include mustard, and some even tuna; some omit the garlic. Good-quality, imported prepared tapenades are now available. One of these can be used in this dish, but choose carefully, using the ingredients listed as a guide when buying. The recipe for the tapenade below yields more than is needed for this dish. The extra can be kept in a glass jar in the refrigerator. Serve it with croutons, hard-boiled eggs, tomatoes, or as an accompaniment to roasted or grilled lamb.

Because of their size it will be difficult to cook more than two cutlets at a time in one skillet, so cook them in two pans or in batches.

FOR THE TAPENADE
⅔ cup niçoise or Greek-type olives, pitted
½ cup capers, rinsed and well drained
3 salted anchovies, rinsed, patted dry, and filleted
1 teaspoon fresh thyme leaves, or ¼ teaspoon dried
10 leaves Italian parsley
Pinch coarse salt
Freshly ground pepper
2 cloves garlic, peeled
4 to 5 tablespoons olive oil

FOR THE CUTLETS
4 pork loin cutlets, each about ⅓ inch thick
Salt
Freshly ground pepper
4 tablespoons tapenade
2 eggs
½ teaspoon olive oil
½ cup freshly grated Parmigiano-Reggiano
Stale breadcrumbs
Peanut, canola, or corn oil for frying
1 lemon, quartered, for serving

Make the tapenade: Combine the olives, capers, and anchovies in the bowl of a food processor fitted with a metal blade and puree. Add the herbs, a small pinch of salt, a generous amount of pepper, and the garlic and continue to process. With the machine running, pour just enough olive oil through the feed tube to produce a medium paste. Makes about 1½ cups.

Make the cutlets: Press the cutlets firmly with the side of a large knife blade to flatten them slightly. Season on both sides with salt and pepper. Spread 1 tablespoon of the tapenade on one side of each cutlet, cover, and place in the refrigerator to firm up the tapenade.

Lightly beat the eggs, olive oil, and a few drops of water in a shallow bowl or a soup plate. Spread the Parmigiano on a plate and a generous amount of breadcrumbs on a large sheet of waxed paper.

Place a cutlet, tapenade side up, on the Parmigiano and sprinkle some of the cheese on the topside, pressing it in lightly with the palm of your hand. Transfer the cutlet to the beaten eggs, spoon some of the egg over the top, and transfer the cutlet swiftly to the breadcrumbs. Sprinkle crumbs generously over the top and press

gently. Leave the cutlet in the crumbs. Repeat with the remaining cutlets and ingredients. The cutlets should remain on the bed of crumbs to dry at room temperature for 1 hour or so before cooking.

Place a large, heavy frying pan over high heat and pour in oil to a depth of ½ inch. When the oil is hot, slip in the cutlets and turn down the heat to medium or medium low if necessary to prevent the cutlets from browning too rapidly. When they are golden around the edges, turn the cutlets with a long-handled spatula. When they are golden and crisp on both sides—after about 8 minutes—transfer the cutlets to paper towels to drain briefly. Serve immediately with the lemon wedges.

SERVES 4

Stuffed Pork Chops

Côtes de Porc Farcies à la Provençale

Other varieties of wild mushrooms can be used in place of the *cèpes,* or cultivated white mushrooms or cremini can be substituted.

3 tablespoons olive oil

1 onion, finely chopped

2 ounces fresh *cèpes,* finely chopped

Leaves of 1 sprig fresh thyme

1 tablespoon fresh rosemary leaves, chopped

2 tablespoons Italian parsley leaves, finely chopped

1 clove garlic, finely chopped

A few drops lemon juice

Salt

Freshly ground pepper

Freshly grated nutmeg

1 egg

½ cup or more fresh breadcrumbs

4 double-rib pork chops, trimmed of all but a thin layer of fat

2 to 3 tablespoons dry white wine

For the stuffing: Place a medium skillet over medium heat, add 1 tablespoon of the olive oil to warm, and then the onion.

Lower the heat and cook the onion until softened but not colored, about 10 minutes. Add the mushrooms, raise the heat to high, and sauté until nearly all the liquid from the mushrooms has evaporated, about 5 minutes. Add the herbs, garlic, lemon juice, and salt, pepper, and nutmeg to taste. Turn the mushroom mixture into a bowl and let it cool for a few minutes. Add the egg and then the breadcrumbs gradually, to make a thick but not overly dry mixture. Combine thoroughly. If the mixture seems too wet, add more crumbs.

Using a small, sharp-pointed knife, pierce the back of each chop deeply, ¾ inch from the spine end to ¾ inch from the tip, to form a pocket. Stuff the pockets with the mushroom mixture, dividing it equally and pushing it in a bit from the open edge of the chops. Close each opening with 2 crossed toothpicks. Season the chops with salt and pepper.

Place a heavy skillet or sauté pan, large enough to hold the chops comfortably in a single layer, over medium heat. Add the remaining 2 tablespoons olive oil. When the oil is hot, add the chops and brown, turning once, about 7 minutes on each side. Cover, reduce the heat to very low, and cook until the chops are tender, about 45 minutes. Turn the chops in their juices several times; if the juices seem to be drying up, add the wine by the tablespoon as needed.

Serve the chops with the pan juices spooned over them.

SERVES 4

Lemongrass Pork Chops

Moo Yang Ta-Krai

Charcoal grilling is among the commonest of Thai cooking methods. It gives meat a distinctive flavor and enhances typical seasonings. In place of the chops in this preparation, chunks of boneless pork threaded onto skewers can be used.

Nam pla and the other Thai ingredients can be found in most Asian markets, if not in a well-stocked specialty market or supermarket. The chops can be served with sweet-and-sour sauce, a fruit-based salsa, or another sauce of choice.

2 cloves garlic, peeled and minced
½ teaspoon freshly ground white pepper
2 tablespoons sugar
2 tablespoons *nam pla* (Thai fish sauce)
2 tablespoons soy sauce
1 tablespoon dark (Asian) sesame oil
1 tablespoon cognac, whiskey, or dry
   white wine
2 tablespoons peeled and finely
   chopped lemongrass
1 tablespoon finely chopped scallion,
   white part only
2 tablespoons unsweetened coconut
   milk
4 pork chops, 6 to 8 ounces each

Mix together all of the ingredients with the exception of the pork chops in a shal-

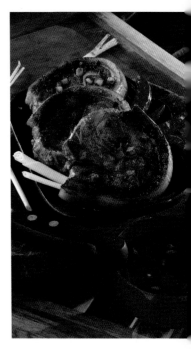

low dish. Wipe the chops and add them to the marinade. Let the chops marinate for about 20 minutes, turning them once or twice.

Meanwhile, prepare a charcoal fire. When the fire is ready, grill the chops for 5 to 6 minutes on each side, or until just cooked through; they should be lightly charred but still slightly pink at the center (they will continue to cook for a minute or so off the heat).

SERVES 4

Cassoulet

Cassoulet refers to the characteristic glazed earthenware dish—a *cassole*—as well as the preparation itself, a country classic that can be found throughout the Languedoc. Some ingredients change from place to place—lamb and partridge are included in Carcassonne; sausage, leg of lamb, and *confit* in Toulouse; stuffed gooseneck and confit in Périgord—but the foundation of dried white beans and a crusty top are consistent wherever cassoulet is found. This version, from Castelnaudary, may be the oldest, and also is among the simplest.

Traditionally, cassoulet is made with beans picked and dried within the year, so try to find the freshest available. Cassoulet is the definitive hearty one-dish meal, and needs only to be followed by a green salad.

1½ pounds dried haricot (white) beans

1 pound ripe tomatoes or 1 28-ounce can good-quality whole canned tomatoes (such as San Marzano), well drained

1 pound lightly salted pork belly

½ pound fresh pork rind, trimmed of all fat

1 pound Toulouse or similar coarse-textured fresh sausage

1 unsmoked kielbasa sausage

8 cloves garlic, peeled

1 teaspoon dried thyme

Salt

Freshly ground pepper

1½ pounds fresh pork tenderloin, bones removed and reserved

1 bouquet garni: 1 bay leaf, 1 sprig fresh thyme, and 6 sprigs parsley

3 medium onions, peeled

2 whole cloves

2 medium leeks, root ends trimmed and all but about 1 inch green top cut away, thinly sliced and carefully washed

6 ounces (12 tablespoons) goose fat, rendered fresh pork fat, butter, or vegetable oil

1 to 2 cups dried white breadcrumbs

Place the beans in a pot and cover generously with cold water. Soak overnight or for at least 4 hours. Or, bring the water to a boil, add the beans, and boil for 2 minutes; remove from the heat, cover, and set aside for 1 hour.

Bring a pot of water to a boil, drop in the tomatoes, and blanch for 10 to 30 seconds. Transfer to a bowl of ice water. Peel the tomatoes, cut them in half, squeeze out the juice and seeds, and coarsely chop the flesh. Set the tomatoes aside.

Bring the water back to a boil, drop in the pork belly and pork rind, and boil for 5 minutes; drain and refresh under cold water. Cut the pork rind into pieces about ¼ inch by 1¼ inches. Prick the Toulouse sausage and the kielbasa all over with a fork to keep them from bursting while cooking.

Cut each of 2 cloves of garlic into 6 slivers. Combine the slivers with the dried thyme and salt and pepper. With a sharp knife, make 12 slits all over the pork tenderloin and slip a seasoned garlic sliver into each. Tie the bouquet garni herbs together with twine or in a piece of cheesecloth.

Finely chop 4 of the remaining garlic cloves. Finely chop 2 of the onions and stud the remaining onion with the cloves.

Drain the beans and discard the water. Return the beans to the pot and cover them with 3 quarts of water. Add the pork belly, leeks, the clove-studded onion, the bouquet garni, pork rind, and the reserved bone from the pork tenderloin. Bring slowly to a boil over low heat; simmer gently for 1½ hours.

Meanwhile, melt half the goose fat in a heavy pot large enough to hold the tenderloin, and brown it on all sides; set the tenderloin aside. Add the chopped onions to the pot and cook over low heat just until golden, about 5 minutes, stirring with a wooden spoon. Add the chopped garlic and cook, stirring, for 2 minutes longer. Add the tomatoes and cook for 3 minutes longer. Season well with salt and pepper. Return the pork tenderloin to the pot, cover, and cook over low heat for 1 hour.

Remove the meat and add it with the ingredients of the pot to the beans. Add the sausages and cook for 30 minutes longer.

Preheat the oven to 375°F.

Remove the meats from the pot and cut them into ¼-inch pieces. Remove the onion and bouquet garni and discard.

Cut the 2 remaining garlic cloves in half and rub them all over the interior of a large ovenproof casserole. Spread a layer of beans on the bottom; cover with a layer of various meats. Continue to layer the ingredients, finishing with a layer of beans. Melt the remaining goose fat and drizzle it over the beans. Sprinkle with breadcrumbs—you should have an even coating about 1/16 inch thick. Place the casserole in the oven. After about 20 minutes, or when the crumbs begin to toast, remove the casserole, and, with the back of a spoon, gently press the crumbs into the liquid at the surface to moisten them. Repeat two or three times as the cassoulet cooks. This is what gives the dish its characteristic and delicious toasty, crusty top. Bake for about 1 hour altogether. The beans and meats should be quite tender. Serve directly from the casserole.

SERVES 8 TO 10

Parsleyed Ham

Jambon Persillé

The name translates to "parsleyed ham," a fairly mundane description for a dish that is a star in the category of cured pork dishes. This is a jellied dish, similar to *tête de veau* in that bits of meat are suspended in gelatin. Here, the pink ham is set off by bright green herbs. The traditional centerpiece of Easter Sunday dinners in Burgundy, this classic dish is perfect for any buffet or luncheon party. If your ham is not particularly salty, you can cut the soaking time in the first step or eliminate it altogether. Typical garnishes are gherkins and mayonnaise.

2 pounds boned smoked ham

2 calf's feet

A 10-ounce veal knuckle or 2 pounds veal bones

2 shallots, cut in half

1 clove garlic, cut in half

1 sprig fresh thyme

1 bay leaf, fresh if possible

2 sprigs fresh tarragon

3 sprigs fresh chervil

3 sprigs Italian parsley

Salt

Freshly ground pepper

3 cups white Burgundy wine

2 tablespoons white wine vinegar

1 cup Italian parsley leaves

leaves from 3 tarragon sprigs

leaves from 3 chervil sprigs

3 scallions, white parts only

Place the ham in a bowl deep enough to hold it comfortably when completely covered with water. Add cold water to cover and soak for 12 to 24 hours, depending on the saltiness of the ham (a traditional country ham will need longer), changing the water at least 3 times.

When ready to prepare the dish, place the calf's feet in water to cover generously, bring to a boil, boil for 5 minutes, drain, and rinse well under cold water.

Drain the ham and rinse it under cold running water. Combine the calf's feet, ham, and veal knuckle or bones in a large pot; add the shallots, garlic, thyme, bay leaf, tarragon, and chervil and parsley sprigs. Season lightly with salt and pepper and pour in the wine. Bring just to the boil,

lower the heat, and simmer for 2 hours, stirring from time to time. Take care to keep the liquid at a low simmer.

Remove the ham and the veal knuckle from the pot and set aside. Strain the cooking liquid through a fine sieve into a bowl and stir in the vinegar; season to taste with salt and pepper. Let the stock cool until it becomes thick and viscous.

Remove any meat from the veal knuckle and discard the bones. With a fork or your fingers, roughly break the ham into pieces and combine it with the veal. Roughly chop the parsley, tarragon, and chervil leaves with the scallions.

Choose a mold just large enough to accommodate the meat and the liquid. Pour in a layer of stock, let it cool, and then place it in the refrigerator until firmly set. Cover the jelled stock with a layer of meat and sprinkle with some of the parsley mixture. Carefully pour another layer of stock over the meat, sprinkle with the parsley mixture, and again refrigerate until firm. Repeat this layering until all the ingredients have been used, ending with a final addition of stock. Each layer will firm sufficiently in about 20 minutes. An alternative, if more casual method, is to simply mix together the strained cooled cooking liquid and other ingredients and turn them into a mold. Only the effect of the layers will be lost.

Cover the mold and refrigerate for 12 hours before unmolding. Serve in slices, accompanied by a tossed green salad.

SERVES 8 TO 10

Choucroute Garni

This American version of the classic French-Alsatian dish migrated to Texas with Henri Castro, who founded the town of Castroville on the Medina River. In time, French, German, English, Alsatian, and Spanish settlers made their home there.

Choucroute is sauerkraut and choucroute garni is a sumptuous dish of braised sauerkraut with various pork products, some cured, some not. In Castroville's choucroute, the sausages are often cooked separately from the braised sauerkraut and other meats and served with additional potatoes. In any case, choucroute is in the category of home cooking, which means there may be as many variations as there are home cooks. The slow cooking of the sauerkraut, however, is essential to the dish and its success. If possible, get your sauerkraut from a specialty shop. This hearty one-dish meal needs only to be followed by a tossed green salad.

A Johannisberg Riesling is the wine to serve with this.

1 pound pork ribs or chops

1 pound sauerkraut

2 tart green apples, such as Granny Smith, halved, cored, and cut into 8 slices

1 white onion, sliced

2 all-purpose potatoes, unpeeled, cut into 2-inch chunks

1 bay leaf

2 cloves garlic, optional

4 whole cloves

2 teaspoons juniper berries, or 1 table-spoon gin

2 or more cups Johannisberg Riesling

1 pound knockwurst or bratwurst (cooked)

Preheat the oven to 350°F.

Place a sauté pan over high heat, add the pork ribs or chops, and brown well on both sides, turning once; this should take 5 to 6 minutes. Remove the chops to a plate and keep in a warm spot.

Combine half the sauerkraut, apple slices, and onion slices in a large ovenproof casserole or Dutch oven. Top with the potatoes, bay leaf, garlic, if using, cloves, and juniper berries. Arrange the remaining sauerkraut, apples, and onions over the top, and then, finally, add the browned pork. Pour in wine just to cover the ingredients.

Transfer the casserole to the oven and bake until the potatoes and pork are tender and most of the liquid has been absorbed, 1½ to 2 hours.

Approximately 20 minutes before the sauerkraut will be done, add the sausages to the casserole. Alternatively, place the sausages in a saucepan and add water to barely cover; bring to a boil, reduce the heat to medium-low, and simmer until the sausages are heated through, about 15 minutes. Drain.

To serve, arrange the sauerkraut and meats on a large warmed platter.

SERVES 4 TO 6

Pork with Sichuan Preserved Cabbage

Chinese preserved cabbage is prepared with fennel, pepper, licorice root, Chinese cassia, chilies, salt, and some liquors. Its flavor is unique and the variety produced in Fulin, in Sichuan Province, is particularly highly regarded. The taste for Chinese preserved cabbage has broken past the country's borders, and preserved cabbage has been exported widely. You will find it in Chinese markets and in many specialty stores that offer Asian ingredients.

6 ounces Sichuan preserved cabbage

12 ounces pork tenderloin

1 tablespoon light soy sauce

2 tablespoons rice wine or dry sherry

1 tablespoon cornstarch

½ teaspoon sugar

1 slender leek or 2 or 3 scallions, trimmed

3 medium slices peeled fresh ginger

1 to 2 small fresh red chilies, cored and seeded

3 tablespoons lard or vegetable oil

Soak the cabbage in cold water for 1 hour. Drain well and press out as much water as possible. Cut the cabbage into strips about 2½ inches wide.

Slice the pork very thinly across the grain. Stack the slices and cut them into very fine shreds. Place the pork in a glass dish. Whisk together the soy sauce, rice wine, cornstarch, and sugar and pour the mixture over the pork; stir to combine and set aside to marinate for 20 minutes.

Cut the leek in half lengthwise, then cut it, with the ginger and chilies, into fine shreds.

Heat the lard in a wok or heavy skillet until it begins to smoke. Add the pork and cabbage and quickly stir-fry together until the pork looses its color. Push the pork and cabbage to the side of the pan and add the shredded vegetables, stir-frying for 1 minute. Combine the vegetables with the pork and cabbage and add 1 tablespoon water. Adjust the seasonings if necessary. Serve at once with hot rice.

SERVES 4

Roast Leg of Lamb with Merlot Marinade

On Lopez Island off the coast of Washington State, farmers raise lamb in the traditional European manner, feeding it on the tasty grasses that grow windward to the Strait of Juan de Fuca. This meat is a great match with Washington State's world-class Merlot, which is the underpinning of this marinade. It goes without saying that a bottle or two should be on hand to drink with the finished dish as well. Some of the labels to look for are Chinook, Columbia, and Latah Creek.

1 boneless leg of lamb, 4 to 6 pounds
1 tablespoon freshly ground pepper
8 cloves garlic, peeled and minced
Leaves from 4 sprigs fresh rosemary
¼ cup olive oil
2 cups good Washington State Merlot
   (see above) or other full-bodied dry
   red wine
2 teaspoons kosher or coarse sea salt

Rub the lamb all over with the pepper and the minced garlic. Chop half the rosemary and rub it on the lamb.

Place the lamb, olive oil, and Merlot in a glass or stainless steel baking pan or similar container that will hold the meat comfortably. Turn the lamb in the marinade and cover it with the remaining rosemary. Cover the pan and place it in the refrigerator. Marinate overnight, turning the meat occasionally.

Preheat the oven to 350°F. Remove the lamb from the marinade and wipe the rosemary and garlic from the surface. Place the lamb on a rack in a shallow roasting pan and season it well with the salt.

Roast the lamb for 20 minutes per pound, or until the internal temperature reaches 145°F for medium-rare. Transfer the lamb to a cutting board and let it rest for 5 to 10 minutes before carving.

SERVES 8 TO 10

Grilled Butterflied Lamb

Lamb lends itself as easily to grilling as beef does, and a butterflied leg can be thought of as a large thick steak that is more interesting, just as simple, and ideal for a casual dinner party. This recipe from California, with its yogurt-based marinade, reflects traditional Middle Eastern methods.

1 leg of lamb, 5 to 6 pounds, boned
   and butterflied
16 ounces plain yogurt
4 cloves garlic, peeled and crushed
½ cup roughly chopped fresh mint
¼ teaspoon freshly ground pepper

Place the lamb in a shallow ceramic or glass dish. Combine the yogurt, garlic, mint, and pepper. Spread the mixture over both sides of the lamb. Cover and refrigerate overnight. Remove from the refrigerator at least one hour before cooking.

Prepare a charcoal fire and lightly oil the rack. When the fire is ready, place the lamb on the rack and grill over medium heat for about 15 minutes on each side for medium-rare (or longer to taste). Remove the lamb to a cutting board to rest for 10 minutes before slicing.

SERVES 6 TO 8

Provençal Roast Leg of Lamb

Gigot Rôti à la Provençale

For traditionalists, a leg of lamb should always be carved at the table, a ceremony that adds an important dimension to the pleasure of a meal. This exercise will be facilitated if you can persuade your butcher to leave the long leg bone attached. Carve away from yourself, at a sharp bias, nearly parallel to the bone, lifting off thin slices, first from the rounded, fleshy side of the leg, then from the leaner muscle to the other side. Finally, slice off small pieces of meat from the leg end. As each section has a slightly different flavor, texture, and degree of doneness, offer a sampling to each guest.

Pinch of kosher or sea salt
Freshly ground pepper
Pinch of Provençal mixed herbs or
    very small pinches of dried thyme,
    oregano, savory, and marjoram or
    a selection to taste
41 firm cloves garlic, peeled
1 tablespoon dry white wine
1 leg of lamb, about 6 pounds, leg
    bone unsawed, pelvic bone and

superficial fat removed, at room
    temperature
2 tablespoons olive oil
2 carrots, peeled and finely chopped
1 large onion, peeled and finely chopped
1 small celery stalk, trimmed and finely
    chopped
3 cups dry red wine
Pinch of fine salt

In a mortar or small grinder or processor combine the coarse salt, pepper to taste, herbs, and 1 clove of the garlic to form a paste. Stir in the white wine.

With a small sharp knife, cut several deep slits into the lamb leg, on the bias and with

the grain. Open up each slit with your finger and, with a small spoon, insert a bit of the herb mixture. Smear any remaining mixture over the surface of the meat. Rub the leg all over with half the olive oil, cover snugly with plastic wrap, and set aside to marinate at room temperature for 1 hour or so.

Meanwhile, place the remaining 1 tablespoon olive oil in a small saucepan over medium heat. Add the chopped vegetables and cook briefly, then pour in the red wine. Bring to a boil and simmer, uncovered, until reduced by two thirds, or to about 1 cup. Pass the mixture through a sieve into a bowl, pressing on the vegetables with a wooden pestle or the back of a spoon to extract all the liquid. Discard the vegetables.

Preheat the oven to 400°F. Put the lamb in a shallow, oval ovenproof dish. Place the dish in the oven to roast for 10 minutes. Reduce the heat to 350°F and continue to roast the lamb for 20 minutes; reduce the heat again to 325°F. When the leg has been in the oven for a total of 45 minutes, turn the oven off and leave the leg in the oven

to rest for 20 minutes. The lamb will be medium-rare. If you think your oven is very tight, open the door for a few minutes to let the temperature drop, then close it again. Or, keep the door an inch or two ajar with a kitchen towel used as a wedge.

While the leg is resting, in a saucepan cover the remaining garlic cloves with water, add the fine salt, and bring to a boil. Simmer for 15 minutes. Drain, reserving the cooking water. Combine the cooked garlic and the red wine reduction in a small saucepan and gently reheat.

Transfer the leg of lamb to a heated serving platter. Place the roasting pan on the stovetop over high heat and deglaze it with some—or all if necessary—of the reserved garlic cooking liquid, scraping the pan bottom with a wooden spoon until all the brown bits are dissolved. Add the deglazing liquid to the wine reduction and bring it to a boil.

Pour the boiling wine reduction into a warmed bowl. Carve the lamb at the table. After carving, add the juices from the carved leg to the bowl and pass it so that the juices and garlic cloves may be ladled over the lamb on each serving.

SERVES 8

Stuffed Leg of Lamb of Provence

Gigot Farci

It can safely be said that legs of lamb are stuffed and roasted in many parts of France, but the fillings vary considerably from place to place. This one is in the style of Provence.

8 ounces wild mushrooms, such as morels, porcini, or chanterelles, or a combination of wild and cultivated

1 tablespoon butter

2 ounces lean smoked bacon, finely chopped

1 fennel heart, chopped

4 tablespoons combined chopped Italian parsley and fresh chervil, or all parsley

2 pinches dried thyme

3 pinches freshly grated nutmeg

Salt

Freshly ground pepper

1 slice white bread, crusts trimmed

2 cloves garlic, peeled and chopped

1 leg of lamb, 5 to 6 pounds, trimmed and boned (but not butterflied)

1 teaspoon peanut or olive oil

3½ pounds all-purpose potatoes

6 tablespoons (¾ stick) unsalted butter

½ teaspoon dried thyme

Trim the mushroom stems. Brush or wipe the caps clean; chop the mushrooms roughly. Melt the 1 tablespoon of butter in a 9-inch nonstick sauté pan, add the bacon, and lightly brown it for about 2 minutes, stirring with a wooden spoon. Add the fennel, cover, and cook for 2 minutes. Add the mushrooms, the parsley and chervil, thyme, nutmeg, and salt and pepper to taste and cook, partially covered, until the fennel is very tender and all the liquid has evaporated, about 10 minutes.

Grind the bread to coarse crumbs in a food processor. Remove the sauté pan from the heat and mix in the crumbs and 1 of the chopped garlic cloves. Stuff the mixture into the cavity of the leg of lamb and sew the opening closed with kitchen thread. Coat the surface all over with the oil and season well with salt and pepper. With a sharp knife, make very shallow crisscross cuts over the surface of the meat.

Preheat the oven to 450°F. Peel the potatoes, rinse and pat them dry, and cut them into very thin slices. Melt the remaining 1 tablespoon butter in a 13- by 9-inch or similar size baking dish. Add the thyme and remaining garlic. Toss the potatoes in the butter mixture to coat them well. Spread the potatoes evenly in the dish.

Place the leg of lamb, rounded side down, on the bed of potatoes. Roast for 30 minutes. Remove the lamb to a platter, turn the potato slices over, return the lamb, turning it over, and roast 25 minutes more. Turn the oven heat off and let the leg of lamb rest in the oven for 10 minutes before carving. The lamb will be medium-rare.

SERVES 8

Leg of Lamb with Pureed Garlic

Gigot d'Agneau à l'Ail

Yet another Provençal treatment of lamb, this one can be served with white beans or roasted potatoes. Braised fennel or roasted tomatoes also can be added to the menu. Some specialty food stores and butchers sell lamb broth.

1 leg of lamb, about 5 pounds
30 cloves garlic, peeled, 6 cut into slivers and 24 left whole
6 anchovy fillets in olive oil, drained and cut into slivers
3 tablespoons olive oil
1 tablespoon chopped fresh rosemary
2 teaspoons chopped fresh thyme
Salt
Freshly ground pepper
½ cup dry white wine
½ cup lamb or beef broth, plus additional as needed

Preheat the oven to 350°F. Make shallow slits all over the leg of lamb and insert slivers of the garlic and bits of anchovy into each slit. Rub the leg with the oil, the rosemary, and the thyme and season to taste with salt and pepper.

Place the leg of lamb in a roasting pan. Roast for about 1 hour and 20 minutes for medium-rare, or until an instant-read meat thermometer inserted into the thickest part registers 125°F.

Meanwhile, combine the whole garlic cloves, the wine, and stock in a saucepan. Bring to a boil; reduce the heat to medium-low and simmer, uncovered, until the garlic is very soft, 15 to 20 minutes. Transfer the garlic and cooking liquid to a blender and puree until smooth.

When the lamb is done, remove it to a platter. Place the roasting pan on the stovetop over medium-high heat. Add the garlic puree to the juices in the roasting pan and stir to combine.

Add additional broth to thin the mixture to a desired sauce consistency. Taste and adjust the seasoning to taste. Transfer to a serving bowl.

Carve the lamb at the table and pass the garlic sauce.

SERVES 6

Roast Lamb with Buttermilk and Rosemary

Some of the world's best lamb is raised in the United States, though it still seems to be less appreciated here than it is in other parts of the world. Wyoming is one of the states where lamb is raised, and this recipe is from Cheyenne.

1 leg of lamb, about 6 pounds

3 cloves garlic, peeled, 1 cut into fine slivers and 2 crushed

1 tablespoon Dijon mustard

Freshly ground pepper

3 tablespoons olive oil

¼ cup buttermilk

½ cup dry white wine

1½ cups homemade or good-quality commercial beef broth

2 sprigs fresh rosemary

1 tablespoon unsalted butter

Salt

Using a small, sharp knife, cut small slits along the top of the lamb and insert a sliver of garlic into each. Combine the crushed garlic with the mustard, ½ teaspoon freshly ground pepper, the olive oil, and buttermilk, and spread the mixture over the lamb. Let the lamb stand at cool room temperature or in the refrigerator for at least 6 hours, basting and turning it frequently as the marinade runs off. If refrigerated, remove at least 45 minutes before cooking.

Preheat the oven to 400°F.

Remove the lamb from the marinade and place it on a rack in a roasting pan; reserve the marinade. Combine the marinade with the wine and ½ cup of the broth. Pour the mixture into the roasting pan; add the rosemary. Place the pan in the oven and roast for 15 minutes. Reduce the heat to 300F and continue to roast the lamb, 15 minutes per pound for medium-rare. Add the remaining stock to the roasting pan as necessary as the juices evaporate. When the lamb is cooked to taste, remove it from the oven and let it rest on a cutting board for 10 minutes before carving.

Meanwhile, skim off the fat from the pan juices and whisk in the butter. Season the sauce with salt and pepper to taste. Transfer the sauce to a serving bowl, carve the lamb, and pass the sauce at the table.

SERVES 6 TO 8

Minted Lamb Chops with Pear Relish

It is well worth acquiring a good Gewürztraminer wine, preferably from a northwestern American winery, for this recipe. Just a bit is needed for the marinade and the relish, and the remainder will be perfect with the grilled lamb, mint, and pears.

The relish can be made a day or more in advance or while the chops are marinating. If made in advance and refrigerated, bring the relish to room temperature before serving.

¼ cup olive oil

¼ cup Gewürztraminer wine

1 clove garlic, peeled and minced

1 teaspoon minced fresh ginger

¼ teaspoon dried red pepper flakes

1 tablespoon chopped fresh mint

Salt

Freshly cracked pepper

6 thick loin lamb chops

Pear Relish (recipe follows)

Fresh mint sprigs for garnish

Stir together all the ingredients up to the lamb chops, including salt and pepper to taste, in a glass or stainless steel dish large enough to hold the chops comfortably. Add the chops and let them marinate at cool room temperature for an hour or longer, turning once.

Prepare a charcoal fire. Remove the chops from the marinade and season them with salt and pepper to taste.

Grill the chops over medium-hot coals for 2 to 3 minutes on each side for medium-rare, or longer, according to taste. Serve immediately, garnished with the mint sprigs, with the pear relish to the side.

SERVES 6

Pear Relish

2 tablespoons olive or vegetable oil

1 red onion, thinly sliced

3 ripe but firm Bosc or Anjou pears, cored
and diced

¼ cup finely diced red bell pepper

1 teaspoon minced fresh ginger

3 whole star anise

¼ teaspoon ground cinnamon

Pinch dried red pepper flakes

3 tablespoons sugar

2 tablespoons distilled white vinegar

¼ cup Gewürztraminer wine

2 tablespoons fresh lemon juice

Grated zest of 1 lemon

1½ teaspoons salt

⅓ cup minced fresh mint

Heat the oil in a heavy nonreactive or enamel saucepan over medium heat. Add the onion and sauté for about 1 minute. Add the remaining ingredients with the exception of the mint and bring to a low boil. Reduce the heat to a simmer and cook, stirring occasionally, until the mixture is thick and syrupy, 35 to 45 minutes.

Let the relish cool to room temperature, then stir in the mint. Serve at room temperature. The relish will keep, tightly covered, in the refrigerator, for up to 1 week.

YIELD: ABOUT 2 CUPS

Lamb Chops Basque Style

Oregon lamb is moist, tender, and full of flavor. This dish is a variation on a rustic lamb stew cooked by Basque shepherds while tending flocks in eastern Oregon. Like so many other immigrants, these shepherds enriched the food style of the place they came to.

12 shoulder or loin lamb chops, about
  3 pounds total
Salt
Freshly ground pepper
¼ cup olive oil
3 tablespoons minced garlic
2 tablespoons chopped fresh marjoram
¾ teaspoon ground cumin
1 red bell pepper, cored, seeded, and
  cut into thin strips
1 green bell pepper, cored, seeded, and
  cut into thin strips
1 yellow onion, peeled and finely diced
1 cup dry red wine, such as Cabernet
  Sauvignon or Pinot Noir
6 cups (3 pounds) peeled, seeded and
  chopped fresh tomatoes or drained
  canned

Season the lamb chops to taste with salt and pepper. Place a large, heavy skillet over medium-high heat, add the olive oil, and sear the lamb chops, a few at a time, for about 2 minutes per side, or until lightly browned. Transfer to a large plate. When all the chops have been seared, set the plate aside in a warm spot.

Reduce the heat to medium and add the garlic, marjoram, and cumin to the pan. Sauté until the garlic is golden, 2 to 3 minutes, being careful not to burn it.

Add the peppers and onion and sauté just until the onion is translucent, 2 to 3 minutes. Add the red wine and tomatoes and simmer 10 to 12 minutes, to reduce the liquid. Add salt and pepper to taste.

Return the lamb chops to the pan, cover, and simmer the chops in the sauce for 3 to 5 minutes to heat them through. Serve the chops from the pan, accompanied with rice and a loaf of rustic bread.

SERVES 6

Lamb and Artichoke Stew

Ragoût d'Agneau aux Artichauts

Rice pilaf, buttered noodles, or parsleyed steamed potatoes are perfect with this stew. Or new potatoes, boiled in their skins just until still a bit firm, then peeled, can be added to the stew for the last ten minutes of cooking time.

3 tablespoons olive oil

1 slice fresh salt pork (about 3 ounces), cut into lardoons about ½ inch by 1½ inches

3 pounds stewing lamb in 1½- to 2-inch cubes, cut from the shoulder, trimmed of excess fat

Salt

Freshly ground pepper

1 large tomato, peeled, seeded, and coarsely chopped

4 cloves garlic, peeled and crushed

1 cup dry white wine

Bouquet garni of 1 bay leaf, 3 sprigs thyme, and 5 sprigs parsley

4 artichokes, trimmed, quartered, and chokes removed

½ pound pearl onions, peeled (see page 26)

Place a heavy sauté pan over medium heat. Add 2 tablespoons of the olive oil, warm it, then add the lardoons and brown on all sides, about 10 minutes. Use a slotted spoon to remove the lardoons to a plate and set aside. Dry the lamb cubes with paper towels and add them to the pan; season with salt and pepper. Cook the lamb until nicely browned on all sides, about 20 minutes, removing the pieces to a bowl as they are done.

Drain the fat from the pan. Add the tomato, garlic, and wine and raise the heat to high. Stir and scrape the pan bottom with a wooden spoon to dissolve any browned bits. Return the lamb to the pan. Add the bouquet garni, reduce the heat to low, cover, and simmer very gently for 1 hour.

Meanwhile, warm the remaining 1 tablespoon olive oil in a large flameproof earthenware or enameled ironware casserole over low heat. Add the artichokes and the onions and season lightly with salt. Cover and sweat over very gentle heat, shaking the pan from time to time, for 20 minutes. Add the reserved lardoons and the lamb mixture. Cover and continue to simmer, stirring once or twice, over very low heat until the artichokes and the meat are tender, another 20 to 30 minutes. Remove the bouquet garni and serve.

SERVES 4

Lamb with Walnut Stuffing

Kilis Kuşlari

A specialty of southeastern Turkey, this dish's true origins are in Syria. A walnut and meat mixture is rolled up in lamb slices, which are then braised in a mild tomato sauce in the oven. The rolls are sometimes browned in a bit of olive oil before braising, but this step is not critical and can be skipped. Serve this with rice pilaf.

8 slices of lamb from the leg, each about ½ inch thick

FOR THE FILLING
2 tablespoons unsalted butter
1 medium onion, peeled and finely chopped
1 pound ground lamb
2 ripe tomatoes, peeled, seeded, and chopped
⅓ cup chopped toasted walnuts
2 tablespoons chopped fresh Italian parsley

1 teaspoon salt
½ teaspoon ground allspice
½ teaspoon ground cinnamon
½ teaspoon ground cumin
Pinch cayenne pepper

FOR THE SAUCE
½ cup tomato puree
1 cup lamb or chicken broth
2 cloves garlic, peeled and minced
3 bay leaves, fresh if possible

Place the lamb slices between sheets of plastic wrap and pound them to a thickness of about ¼ inch. Refrigerate while you prepare the filling.

For the filling: Place a small saucepan over medium heat, and add the butter, to melt.

Add the onion and sauté until tender and translucent, about 8 minutes; do not let the onion brown. Add the ground lamb, breaking it up with a wooden spoon or fork, and sauté, stirring, until the meat loses its color, about 8 minutes. Add the remaining filling ingredients and cook,

stirring, for about 3 minutes to blend the flavors. Turn the filling into a bowl and allow it to cool to room temperature.

Meanwhile, make the sauce: Combine all the sauce ingredients in a small saucepan and bring to a simmer, stirring. Cover the sauce and keep it on a very low simmer while you assemble the rolls.

Preheat the oven to 350°F.

When the filling is cool, divide it among the slices of lamb, positioning it somewhat off-center and spreading it out, but not all the way to the edges. Roll the slices up,

starting with the edges nearest the filling, and secure the open ends with small skewers, toothpicks, or kitchen twine. Place the rolls, seam side down, in a lightly oiled baking dish that will hold them snugly.

Ladle the sauce over the rolls and transfer the dish to the oven. Bake the rolls, basting them from time to time, until tender, about 1 hour.

Serve the rolls from the baking dish or transfer them to a warmed platter.

SERVES 4

Seared Lamb Loin with Coriander Seed Paste

Fragrant coriander and lamb have a natural affinity for each other. Grilled figs and grilled artichoke hearts would make spectacular accompaniments. Cabernet Sauvignon would be the wine of choice.

3 tablespoons coriander seeds
1½ teaspoons whole peppercorns
5 cloves garlic, peeled
4½ teaspoons Asian fish sauce (*nam pla*)
5 teaspoons soy sauce
2 tablespoons fresh lime juice
1 lamb loin, 1½ pounds
Chives and, if available, chive blossoms, optional, for garnish

In a blender or electric grinder, combine the coriander seeds, peppercorns, garlic, fish sauce, soy sauce, and lime juice and process until the seeds are fully crushed.

Place the lamb loin in a shallow glass or ceramic dish and spread the seed mixture over the entire surface. Cover and refrigerate for at least 6 hours or for up to 24 hours.

Preheat the oven to 350°F.

Wipe away excess marinade from the lamb loin. Place a dry, heavy skillet over medium-high heat. When it is hot, add the lamb and sear it, turning it as needed to brown it richly and evenly on all sides. Transfer the meat to a roasting pan and place the pan in the oven. Roast the lamb to taste, about 20 minutes for medium-rare, or until an instant-read thermometer inserted at the thickest point registers 130 to 140°F.

Transfer the lamb loin to a cutting board and let it rest for 5 minutes. Using a sharp knife, cut it into thick slices and arrange them on a warm serving platter. Garnish with the chives and chive blossoms, if using.

Serves 4

Index

adobo sauce, roast leg of pork in, 80–81
anchovies, roast pork with olives and, 76–77
artichoke and lamb stew, 126–27

bacon, and calf's liver with orange-leek sauce, 62–63
barbecue:
  brisket, best-of-the-border, 53–55
  Korean, 51–52
Barolo wine, beef braised in, 18–19
beef:
  boiled, with chili, 22–23
  braised in Barolo, 18–19
  Burgundy, 24–26
  curry, Sumatran, 27–29
  ground, salad, 47–48
  and potato stew, 20–21
  rolls, stuffed, 43–44
  round, in *carne guisada*, 34–35
  shank, in Provençal pot-au-feu, 38–40
  stout-braised, with onions and sour cream, 30–31
  waterfall, 49–50
beer:
  in best-of-the-border barbecue brisket, 53–55
  in Texas short ribs, 32–33
beets, in New England boiled dinner, 36–37
bell peppers:
  in *carne guisada*, 34–35
  in lamb chops Basque style, 124–25
  in pear relish, 123
  in Texas short ribs, 32–33
best-of-the-border barbecue brisket, 53–55
blue cheese sauce, Oregon flank steak with, 10–11
boiled beef with chili, 22–23
breadcrumbs:
  in cassoulet, 95–97
  in fried meatballs, 41–42
  in pork cutlets with tapenade, 90–91
  in roast lamb of Pauillac, 106–7

in stuffed pork chops, 92–93
brisket, best-of-the-border barbecue, 53–55
buffalo:
  filet with peppercorns and mustard, 70–71
  steak, marinated, 68–69
Burgundy beef, 24–26
buttermilk:
  roast lamb with rosemary and, 119–20
  in steak verde with crisp pepper-fried onion shreds, 12–14

cabbage:
  in New England boiled dinner, 36–37
  Sichuan preserved, pork with, 102–3
calf's feet, in parsleyed ham, 98–99
calf's liver:
  and bacon with orange-leek sauce, 62–63
  harvesters', 64–65
capers, in pork cutlets with tapenade, 90–91
carne guisada, 34–35
cassoulet, 95–97
Catalonian pork brochettes, 84–85
Chianti, steak marinated in, 6–7
chili, boiled beef with, 22–23
chilies, *see specific chilies*
chipotle-cranberry sauce, pork tenderloin with, 78–79
choucroute garni, 100–101
cilantro, in sweet and savory pork leg with rice, 82–83
coconut milk:
  in pork curry, 89
  in Sumatran beef curry, 27–29
cognac, in braised veal shank with herbs, 58–59
cranberry-chipotle sauce, pork tenderloin with, 78–79
curry, pork, 89

Dijon mustard:
  buffalo filet with peppercorns and, 70–71

flank steak with Oregon blue cheese sauce, 10–11
Florentine steak, 4
fried meatballs, 41–42

garlic:
  leg of lamb with puréed, 117–18
  tomatoes, and oregano sauce, steaks with, 15
goose fat, in cassoulet, 95–97
grilled:
  butterflied lamb, 112
  porterhouse, 2–3
ground beef salad, 47–48

ha cha cha sauce, rib eye steaks with frizzled onions and, 8–9
ham, parsleyed, 98–99
haricot beans, in cassoulet, 95–97
harvesters' calf's liver, 64–65
heavy cream, in veal stew with mushrooms and peas, 60–61

kaffir lime leaves, in pork curry, 89
ketchup, in best-of-the-border barbecue brisket, 53–55
Korean barbecue, 51–52

lamb:
  and artichoke stew, 126–27
  grilled butterflied, 112
  loin, seared with coriander seed paste, 130
  roast, of Pauillac, 106–7
  roast, with buttermilk and rosemary, 119–20
  shank, in Provençal pot-au-feu, 38–40
  with walnut stuffing, 128–29
  see also leg of lamb
lamb chops:
  Basque style, 124–25
  minted, with pear relish, 121–23
  leek-orange sauce, calf's liver and bacon with, 62–63
leg of lamb:
  marinated grilled, 108–9

with puréed garlic, 117–18
  roast, with Merlot marinade, 110–11
  stuffed, of Provence, 115–16
lemongrass pork chops, 94
lemon juice, in Texas short ribs, 32–33
lettuce, in boiled beef with chili, 22–23

Maggi seasoning, in sweet and savory pork leg with rice, 82–83
marinated:
  buffalo steak, 68–69
  grilled leg of lamb, 108–9
marjoram, steak with mushrooms and, 16–17
marrowbone, in Provençal pot-au-feu, 38–40
meatballs, fried, 41–42
meat Uruapan style, 88
Merlot marinade, roast leg of lamb with, 110–11
minted lamb chops with pear relish, 121–23
molasses, in ha cha cha sauce, 8–9
Monterey Jack cheese, in steak verde with crisp pepper-fried onion shreds, 12–14
mushrooms:
  steak with marjoram and, 16–17
  veal stew with peas and, 60–61

New England boiled dinner, 36–37
nuts, in Sumatran beef curry, 27–29

olives, roast pork with anchovies and, 76–77
onion(s):
  frizzled, rib eye steaks with ha cha cha sauce and, 8–9
  shreds, crisp pepper-fried, steak verde with, 12–14
  stout-braised beef with sour cream and, 30–31
orange-leek sauce, calf's liver and bacon with, 62–63

oregano, tomato, and garlic
 sauce, steaks with, 15

Parmigiano-Reggiano, in pork
 cutlets with tapenade,
 90–91
parsleyed ham, 98–99
pasilla chilies, in roast leg of
 pork in adobo sauce, 80–81
pear relish, minted lamb chops
 with, 121–23
peas, veal stew with mushrooms and, 60–61
pepper:
 cracked black, in flank steak
  with Oregon blue cheese
  sauce, 10–11
 -fried onion shreds, crisp,
  steak verde with, 12–14
 steak, 4
peppers, *see specific peppers*
pig's foot, in Provençal
 pot-au-feu, 38–40
Pinot Noir, in flank steak with
 Oregon blue cheese
 sauce, 10–11
poblano chili(es):
 in steak verde with crisp
  pepper-fried onion shreds,
  12–14
 in stuffed meat loaf with
  salsa de jitomate, 45–46
pork:
 brochettes, Catalonian,
  84–85
 in choucroute garni,
  100–101
 curry, 89
 cutlets with tapenade,
  90–91
 lard, in beef braised in
  Barolo, 18–19
 leg, sweet and savory, with
  rice, 82–83
 rind, in cassoulet, 95–97
 roast leg of, in adobo sauce,
  80–81
 with rosemary, 74–75
 with Sichuan preserved
  cabbage, 102–3
 skewered roasted, with malt
  sugar, 86–87
 in stuffed meat loaf with
  salsa de jitomate, 45–46
 tenderloin, in cassoulet,
  95–97
 tenderloin with cranberry-
  chipotle sauce, 78–79
 see also salt pork

pork chops:
 lemongrass, 94
 stuffed, 92–93
porterhouse, grilled, 2–3
potato and beef stew, 20–21
Provençal pot-au-feu, 38–40
Provençal roast leg of lamb,
 113–14
prunes, venison stew with,
 66–67

red wine:
 in harvesters' calf's liver,
  64–65
 in lamb chops Basque style,
  124–25
 in marinated buffalo steak,
  68–69
 in pork tenderloin with
  cranberry-chipotle sauce,
  78–79
 in Provençal roast leg of
  lamb, 113–14
 in steak with mushrooms
  and marjoram, 16–17
 in stuffed beef rolls, 43–44
 in venison stew with prunes,
  66–67
rib eye steaks with ha cha cha
 sauce and frizzled onions,
 8–9
ribs, *see* short ribs
rice, sweet and savory pork leg
 with, 82–83
roast:
 lamb of Pauillac, 106–7
 lamb with buttermilk and
  rosemary, 119–20
 leg of lamb with Merlot
  marinade, 110–11
 leg of pork in adobo sauce,
  80–81
 pork with olives and
  anchovies, 76–77

salad, ground beef, 47–48
salsa de jitomate, stuffed meat
 loaf with, 46
salt pork:
 in beef and potato stew,
  20–21
 in Burgundy beef, 24–26
 in cassoulet, 95–97
 in lamb and artichoke stew,
  126–27
sauerkraut, in choucroute
 garni, 100–101
sausage:
 in cassoulet, 95–97

in choucroute garni, 100–101
seared lamb loin with coriander seed paste, 130
short ribs:
 in Provençal pot-au-feu,
  38–40
 Texas, 32–33
skewered pork roasted with
 malt sugar, 86–87
sour cream, stout-braised beef
 with onions and, 30–31
soy sauce:
 in Korean barbecue, 51–52
 in sweet and savory pork leg
  with rice, 82–83
 in Yangnyum Kanjang sauce,
  52
spinach:
 in pork curry, 89
 in stuffed beef rolls, 43–44
steak(s):
 flank, with Oregon blue
  cheese sauce, 10–11
 Florentine, 4
 marinated buffalo, 68–69
 marinated in Chianti, 6–7
 with mushrooms and
  marjoram, 16–17
 pepper, 4
 rib eye, with ha cha cha
  sauce and frizzled onions,
  8–9
 with tomato, garlic, and
  oregano sauce, 15
 verde with crisp pepper-fried
  onion shreds, 12–14
stew:
 beef and potato, 20
 lamb and artichoke, 126–27
 veal, with mushrooms and
  peas, 60–61
 venison, with prunes, 66–67
stout-braised beef with onions
 and sour cream, 30–31
stuffed:
 beef rolls, 43–44
 leg of lamb of Provence,
  115–16
 meat loaf with *salsa de
  jitomate,* 45–46
 pork chops, 92–93
Sumatran beef curry, 27–29
swamp cabbage, in pork curry,
 89
sweet and savory pork leg with
 rice, 82–83

tamarind juice, in pork curry,
 89

tapenade, pork cutlets with,
 90–91
Texas short ribs, 32–33
Thai fish sauce:
 in pork curry, 89
 in waterfall beef, 49–50
tomatoes:
 garlic, and oregano sauce,
  steaks with, 15
 in *salsa de jitomate,* 45–46
 in Texas short ribs, 32–33
turnips:
 in New England boiled
  dinner, 36–37
 in Provençal pot-au-feu,
  38–40

veal:
 knuckle, in parsleyed ham,
  98–99
 stew with mushrooms and
  peas, 60–61
veal shank(s), braised:
 with herbs, 58–59
 with lemon, 56–57
vegetables, in waterfall beef,
 49–50
venison stew with prunes,
 66–67

walnut stuffing, lamb with,
 128–29
waterfall beef, 49–50
white wine:
 in choucroute garni,
  100–101
 in lamb and artichoke stew,
  126–27
 in leg of lamb with puréed
  garlic, 117–18
 in minted lamb chops with
  pear relish, 121–23
 in parsleyed ham, 98–99
 in pork with rosemary,
  74–75
 in Provençal pot-au-feu,
  38–40
 in roast lamb with buttermilk and rosemary,
  119–20
 in roast pork with olives and
  anchovies, 76–77
 in veal stew with mush-
  rooms and peas, 60–61

Yangnyum Kanjang sauce, 52
yogurt, in grilled butterflied
 lamb, 112